© 2025 A.T. Garcia

All rights reserved. No part of this book may be reproduced, stored, or transmitted in any form or by any means without the prior written permission of the author.

This memoir is based on true events; some details have been changed to protect the

privacy of individuals.

Published by Kiffer Book Club

Texas, USA

ISBN: 979-8-9993745-0-9

Cover design by A.T. Garcia

Printed in the United States of America

The Clothes on My Back

A.T. Garcia

The Magical Fields

My mama was a runner. She ran from her dad, ran from her friends, and ran from her life. She ran from her kids and ran from her job. She ran from everything that threatened her peace, and she rarely ever looked back.

As a child, I'd sit and wonder why she ruined our peace, which was the very definition of a lifestyle that was not peaceful, but we didn't know. All we really knew was the woman who stood with us in that wide, empty field.

She stood quietly, her soft smile catching the sunlight, her pale skin dotted with freckles, long dark hair lifting in the breeze as my brother and I picked dandelions and ran after wild rabbits. She watched us with eyes full of something tender and faraway. She fed our imaginations like they were the only thing that mattered and told us stories of fairies in the clover and hidden rewards waiting just beneath the petals.

And we believed her.

She laughed silly with us and let us believe that the world was full of magic and play.

She held our hands and spun us around as we squealed in delight. I saw images like a kaleidoscope of the grass and terrain as she flung me round and round before gently setting me down. "Again!" I cried.

She was the sunlight that shone on our young faces, and the wind that carried us along. She was the whispers that put us gently to sleep, and the songs that we sang on our walks. She was the shoulder I lay on when I was tired. She was our answer to everything.

Back then, she wasn't a woman weighed down by shame and poor choices. She was just a girl of twenty-one, alone and unsure, lost and fragile; she was our young mama, and we loved her.

Hard Times at the East Side High

I sat in school one day and silently pleaded with the teacher not to call on me. I was quiet, withdrawn, and afraid of the sound of my own voice. I attempted my best impression of an invisible student. Years of emotional bruising left me feeling unsure of everything I said or did, like one more shitstorm in that school would cause me to mentally collapse. At that point in my life, thinking about the future felt laughable. I was a teenager just trying to survive the day in that rundown, half-condemned neighborhood my dad so proudly moved us to, like he'd won the damn lottery. Survival became the goal. Hope became too far to reach.

I heard the teacher pace nearby, and when I glanced up, she was staring down at my pointless doodling on my desk. Her name was Ms. Yelverton from Ithaca, New York, and she was far from home. She took an assignment no sane college grad would even touch. But she was different. She *wanted* to be in our mess. She cared enough to stick her nose where most people wouldn't dare, because she saw something in a pocket of pain the rest of the world had written off. She recognized it because she carried it too. She'd left an abuser behind, and the scars she hid made her see ours more clearly. She hurt, and somehow, some way, being there for us became therapeutic to her healing.

The class discussion for that day was on bad leadership. It went from high-school students bitching about their managers at their first jobs, to complaining about bad teachers. I had undiagnosed ADHD and didn't realize I was the only one who hadn't spoken. Oblivious, as usual, just lost in my own head until it was too late.

My only friend was Luci, an immigrant from Mexico who was just as pretty as she was smart. She spoke very little English, and it boggled my mind why she ended up at a foundry school like this one.

"What about you?" Ms. Yelverton asked me in her inquisitive, high-pitched voice.

I grew up in the kind of poverty you wouldn't think still existed in the 90s. Not at that level. And definitely not in such a big, growing city. Much of the poverty was caused by my parents, but it existed hidden in plain sight, conveniently ignored.

Without considering the consequences, I blurted out how unpleased I was with my own home, and that the "landlord" was my dad's parents. Ms. Yelverton pressed for details until she saw me visibly uncomfortable, shaking, and turning bright red. I kept my eyes down as I spoke, careful not to let anyone see the frustration I felt. I briefly described how the toilet was falling through the floor of the bathroom, and no one bothered to fix it. I went on about the broken windows and no heat for cold winters. I hoped I would shut up already, but I didn't know how. Maybe I needed to vent. I wasn't sure. But I felt that she was expecting me to share something, and I didn't know what to say. I cringed at the reality that I kept speaking.

Shut the hell up already! The damage was done. When it finally ended and class went out for break, Luci looked at me and said, "Wow, your face turned red like a tomato!" I was humiliated.

Puppy Love

My entire teenage life was mostly filled with chaos and despair. I spent all those years planning and practicing running away. I was naïve and afraid, but I had lost all love and respect for my father, the most.

He was a broken man, addicted to drugs, alcohol, and women. When he was kind, he was kind. When he was high, he was the biggest asshole. It was a sweltering day in August, and being twelve felt like a line in the sand, like I was stepping into the world of growing up. I had my first awkward kiss that summer, a boy held my hand, and I watched my older cousins experiment with makeup and use training bras. But while I was figuring out what it meant to grow up, he was showing me what it meant to be a monster. I stopped looking at him like a father that summer and started seeing him for what he was. A careless, corrupted, selfish heathen, who never wanted anything to do with me.

But I also got my first puppy, which would end up being my first love.

It must've been a Saturday or Sunday, and my dad was throwing a backyard BBQ. We lived on about an acre of land in a very busted house with poor landscape, but that didn't stop him. He invited all his buddies and a few relatives for the usual ritual of drinking, smoking weed, and eating. They all took turns grilling and preparing food. I remember how happy it made me feel when my cousins would come over. We'd slip into our own little world, trading stories, laughing, and having the kind of conversations that felt like secrets. We'd watch the drunks behave foolishly and make fun of them from the sidelines.

We had fun on a go-kart my dad made from scratch out of a lawn mower engine, and we'd ride it around the long dirt road at full speed, drifting across the road, making the dirt and gravel fly up above us. I could still hear the cries of approval from my dad's friends as we circled back to the gate.

But the joy would soon be met with melancholy, and it was all my fault. I just wanted to explore and feel a little grown. My dad wasn't exactly the kind of person who would warn me about the dangers that lurked in the world. So, when my cousin asked if we could walk to the corner store, about 3 blocks away, no one questioned it.

I had to leave my pup inside. I remember feeling a little guilty, so I made us an ice cream cone and let her have the first few licks.

My cousin laughed, "Ew! Did you really let the dog eat that?" I just shrugged. I loved that puppy so much. It felt like she was the only one I really had.

My cousin grew impatient and flung the screen door open, expecting me to follow. I quickly tossed my ice cream, rubbed the puppy's head, and walked out of the house behind her, listening to my dog whine. I remember feeling sad and wanting to hurry back.

I can't remember anything about the walk with my cousin or what we talked about. The only part I remember is arriving home. Upon reaching the entry point of the long dirt road, we saw my aunt leaving in her black Oldsmobile and turning the corner very fast. My cousin and I exchanged glances, and she wondered where her mother was off to so quickly. When we arrived at the house, everyone was standing around, watching me as I walked into the house.

I don't remember who told me, or how exactly, but I heard someone utter the most awful words I had ever heard at that time, about how when the door opened, the dog ran out to chase me and was hit in the street. She did not survive.

The rest of that evening was blurry, and I couldn't come out of my room. I remember being curled up on the floor, playing my dog's favorite song on cassette over and over, for what seemed an eternity, and I didn't have any plans to move. One by one, hour after hour, guests left, and a few of them even peeked in through my curtain door to say bye. My aunt tried explaining that she sped away, trying to take the puppy to the vet for help, but it was too late.

Once most guests were gone, my drunk ass dad decided to find a way to keep the party vibe going by dismissing the excruciating heartache I was feeling.

He leaned his fat head into my room through the curtain and said, "Hey, I know you're sad, but I never liked that little dog anyway."

Yes. He really said that. He actually fucking said that.

I played it over and over in my head, trying to unbelieve that he said that to me. I wanted to shout obscenities at him, but my twelve-year-old self was still too afraid of him, so I replied with a weepy "I hate you".

And I did. I hated him with every bone in my body and every hair on my head.

Run, Me, Run

I became a runner. I learned from the best. I witnessed my mother running from everyone under the sun. She ran from her drunk ass dad, and she ran from my drunk ass dad. She ran from the police, and she ran from the church. And then she ran from me. Maybe she didn't even know she was running anymore.

But I did.

And I wanted to run too.

Sometimes, my imagination got the best of me, and took me far away from everything I knew, just like when I was a kid, the way my mom made me believe in the most peculiar things. She always made me believe there was something better out there, or some life where we'd be accepted, loved, and safe. And honestly, that's all I ever wanted. That was all I was searching for.

When my dad went to work, I ran away. When my dad went to bed or to get high for the night, I ran away. I kept doing it until I got comfortable. I was preparing myself to leave. I didn't know where. I didn't have a plan, but I wanted to leave him. I wanted to go somewhere better and far away from this shitty place.

By this time, things had gotten so bad that we didn't have running water in the house for weeks. We didn't have electricity. We didn't have a working phone line. My older brother figured out how to use calling cards so we could still talk to friends, but I think, deep down, he was still hoping our mom would call. That she'd come back to us. But by then, she was already long gone.

My dad stopped paying the utilities periodically. He was depressed. He couldn't. He was paying out the ass in fines from DUIs and wrecked cars. He spent what was left at the bars. The food we ate was leftover airplane food from his job in the days when they served microwavable pizzas and macaroni and cheese in flight. Some nights, he'd bring us home fast-food burgers after all the bars closed. Living with him was trash. I had no more reason to stay. I would run away for a few days, and get picked up by the police and returned right back home.

No one wanted me. I had a few trips to group homes and children's shelters, and yet my dad never cleaned up the mess. He never saw the problem.

One night, I took off with a group of runaways I'd met on the streets, kids about my age, sharper in their street smarts, tougher from experience. They knew how to survive in ways I hadn't learned yet. But they didn't care about me—not really.

We were loitering outside a store, restless and aimless, when the police suddenly rolled up. Panic scattered us like birds from a wire. Everyone bolted in different directions.

I tried to keep up, but my legs felt heavy with fear. "Green Eyes," as she called herself, glanced back at me for a split second. There was a flicker of worry in her expression, something almost like concern. But then she disappeared into the night.

I was still staring after her when the officers stepped in front of me, cutting off my escape. I froze, heart pounding, caught in their headlights and the harsh weight of reality.

I sat in the back, staring blankly ahead, replaying every decision that led me to this moment. My mind kept circling the same questions: Why did I feel so desperate to leave home? What was so unbearable that I chose this life of running, hiding, surviving on scraps—over the roof and family I once had? Was it really that bad? And if it was, was this any better?

Eventually, I was placed in a children's shelter. What felt almost surreal, or cruel, was that my aunt on my dad's side worked there. We shared an uncommon name, one she would've recognized instantly. She knew I was there. I was sure of it.

But she never came.

Not to check on me. Not to offer help. Not even to say a single word.

Instead, she chose to shame my father, already the black sheep of the family, by telling everyone where I had ended up. Not to rally support or concern, but to highlight the mess, to add weight to his failures.

Maybe it was for the best. Maybe her silence, her absence, was the clearest sign that I didn't belong—

not just at home, but even in the places where family was supposed to mean something.

After checking me in and asking a few routine questions, the staff offered me something to eat. It was late, and the only thing they had left was a Cup O' Noodles. I was starving; it might as well have been a feast.

I sat there struggling to twirl the noodles with a plastic fork, but they kept slipping off, falling back into the cup like they were mocking me. That's when the social worker noticed and quietly handed me a spoon. She smiled gently and showed me a trick, something that felt like a revelation to me at the time, but probably second nature to most people.

She taught me to scoop the noodles onto the spoon and then twirl the fork inside it. It actually worked.

I devoured them.

Something about that small moment stuck with me. It was not just the food, but the kindness in it. The quiet way she saw me struggling, and helped without making me feel small. I smiled slightly, a little embarrassed, but I didn't have to be.

After about a week at the shelter and attending the on-campus school a few times, I met a girl who said she was planning to run away. She told me I was probably too young to come with them, but that she and the other girls ran all the time. According to her, they didn't need anything clever or sneaky; they just walked out the front door at night.

But I couldn't go. I was placed in a room with younger kids, some as young as six. They were sweet and curious, full of questions, like I was some kind of older sibling they didn't know they needed. They even asked me to stay.

They didn't seem to know what a loving home felt like, either, but they had the shelter. They had each other. And I... I had the memory of my dysfunctional home, the one I left behind.

Then one day, my dad showed up.

The second I saw him, fear took over. I braced myself for the worst. Maybe some shouting, guilt, maybe even a hit once we got in the car. But it didn't come. He was quiet. Something in him seemed different. Maybe it was the shame my aunt had stirred up by telling the family. Or maybe he'd just given up. I couldn't tell.

He had one of my dogs with him, a dog I had always loved deeply. We called her Clementine. But I hadn't realized how much she loved me, too. Not until she saw me.

She went wild with joy, her whole body shaking with excitement. And something in me cracked. I knelt down and wrapped my arms around her as tears welled up in my eyes. I didn't know if I was crying because I missed her, because I felt loved for the first time in a while, or because I was heading back to the place I had run from. Maybe it was all of it.

The ride home, I kept waiting for my dad to blow up at me. He didn't know how to parent anyone. The few times he expressed concern were the times he thought beating me with the nearest object would teach me a lesson, but it didn't. It made me hate him more.

Go ahead and beat me like you did my mom. Look where she's at. She left you, and I will too.

In a Different World

I knew from a young age that I came with quirks. I was impulsive, wildly defiant, and painfully awkward when it came to people. By the time I was five, I had already lived in more places than most people do in a lifetime.

There were homeless shelters with my young, tired mother—places with fluorescent lights, crinkly mattresses, and a rotation of faces that never stuck around. When we overstayed our welcome, we ended up in budget motels that smelled like stale French fries and decades of cigarette smoke. We couch-surfed for a while. Some places were rough, others weirdly magical. But the nicest place by far was my Aunt Cathy's house.

She married my uncle and somehow put up with him for years, but to me, she was the definition of *family*. She had two kids, my cousins, and they lived a life that felt like it had fallen straight out of a TV show. I used to think they were rich. Not because they had anything fancy, but because everything they had was *stable*.

My cousin, Millie, was a cheerleader, played volleyball, and could actually play the piano without smashing the keys like I did. At family parties, she'd serenade us with real songs. I thought she was famous. My other cousin, Gus, was a daredevil on a dirt bike, zooming through fields like a superhero. He'd take me riding sometimes, and I'd laugh so hard my stomach would hurt. And there were always parties, with tons of food and people. No one ever missed a gathering at Aunt Cathy's house. To them, it was just their life. To me, it was everything. It was a glimpse of what childhood *could* be. If they had adopted me, I think I would've stayed forever.

My aunt understood the struggles I was going through as a kid. She did what she could to give me a sense of normalcy whenever I stayed with her, even though there were limits to how much she could help. She couldn't step in without upsetting my uncle or offending my deadbeat parents, and if she crossed that line, she might've lost the little time we had together. But she saw me. She knew I was hiding things I was ashamed of. She could see the signs of what would later be called ADHD, OCD, and PTSD. She didn't need a diagnosis to know I was struggling. She just knew, and it didn't stop her from adoring me. She cared about me when I was a lost child, a bad child, and a good child, which probably wasn't often.

Aunt Cathy never made a scene if my clothes were dirty or my hair was a mess. In a lifetime of disappointment, she was the one person who never let me down.

The House That Needed Jesus

I learned to pray when I was young, and by the time I was a teenager, it was all I had to hold onto. There was no one else. I used to ache for a mother or father who would just sit beside me, hold me, and say, *It's going to be okay.* But that was just another mirage, something I made up, something to hope for. I ran away almost every week, hoping to find something, anything, that felt like safety or love. But I never did. All I found was more trouble, more pain, more mistakes that left marks I couldn't erase. The world doesn't cradle kids like me; it devours them, swallows them whole like a crumb before they even realize that's all that they are.

I must have been a preschool-age kid, definitely younger than five, when my dad brought my brother and me to live with his parents. He traveled a lot for work, cleaning planes, living his best life, and he didn't like having kids with him on the road. My mother was in no position to care for us either. Most of the time, she didn't even have a place to live.

My dad had ten siblings, many of them still teenagers back then, and living among them was its own kind of hell. They were loud, mean, foul-mouthed, and just some of the most awful people I've ever had to be around. All except for one aunt, Hanna. She was different.

It was miserable living there. I can still hear the small engine plane flying over from outside, through the small window as we sat on the small bed in the small room of that God awful house. It was the only sign of the outside world my brother and I would see for days on end. The engine would gradually get louder, we'd rush to the window, and stare out until it slowly faded away. Our only stimulus for the day.

In the mornings, my grandparents would unlock the door to let the girls get ready for school in the room and check our bed sheets. That's when I would catch a glimpse of a painting on the wall in the back hall near the door, of a child, about my age, kneeling and praying, with a glowing light shining down on her. It looked hopeful and promising. I tried my best to replicate that moment, praying to a God no one really explained to me, thinking maybe someone other than people would hear my cries for help.

It didn't happen overnight. Days went by of loneliness and isolation, sitting in that room, waiting to be fed, waiting for acknowledgement, waiting for a drink, waiting for a bathroom break. None of which ever came in time. By the time my grandparents opened that door bright and early in the morning, the sheets were already wet. Someone was going to get hit.

I got so sick and tired of watching my brother, a year older than me, wail and scream from getting whipped with a belt for soiling the bed, that I started doing the same, just to offload some of the pain away from him.

My face was pressed firmly against the mattress by my aunt when my grandparents yanked my pants down, asked me which belt we were using today, and whipped me swiftly across the bare bottom until I screamed at the top of my lungs from how bad it stung. The whippings were repeated at least five or six times, but it felt like a hundred, and I never knew if more were coming. As soon as I'd catch my breath, another whip would come out of nowhere. Even when my brother wasn't the one getting hit, he still flinched, cried, and screamed with me, and I saw his face turn red as his cheeks became soaked with tears. Every night, I assured him that we were going to find a way out and run away. It didn't even occur to me how little we were.

And each day, there were subtle signs of hope that kept my little mind going. Out of boredom, I found challenges, and sometimes even victories. I learned to tie a shoe. I spent hours with an old sneaker I found under the bed, playing with its laces until one day—I tied them right. When I felt confident, I taught my brother how to do it. It was a small thing, but it felt like proof I could figure things out, that I had determination, that I could be something.

Then there was my uncle Austin, my dad's younger brother, who had a mischievous streak to him. He would shove a bag of Cheerios through the two-inch gap under the door. It always felt like a secret gift. And when my grandparents were out picking or cleaning offices, he'd sneak us outside to play. He was bratty as he was chunky, always teasing us, and often acted like a shithead, but freedom was worth the price, and we gladly paid it. Maybe it was kindness. But I think he was really lonely.

Whenever we heard voices or footsteps near the door, we'd press close to the crack, hearts racing, trying to see if it was him. Maybe this time he'd let us out again. Maybe not. But even the *maybe* was enough to keep us waiting. It was enough to keep us hoping.

At some point, I started getting on my knees, trying to be that little girl from the painting, the one with the angelic glow on her face, hands clasped, eyes turned up toward the heavens like she had God's direct line. I didn't know any actual prayers, so I just squeezed my hands tight and whispered, "Please, God, call my mama for us." It was less prayer, more desperate request to the heavenly customer service line.

Night after night, I tried. Same pose. Same tiny, pleading voice. But nothing. Not even a ghost of her voice came through. Maybe the call was on hold.

Then, one early morning, my brother and I were jolted awake, not by monsters, for once, but by yelling. Not the usual kind. This was *her* voice. Our mom. She was outside the room with our teenage Uncle Roy, who was more bark than bite but always full of drama. There was scuffling, then a scream, "Open the fucking door!" followed by a loud *THUD*. My brother and I looked at each other, eyes wide, and immediately began shadowboxing the air like tiny warriors, whispering, "Get him! Get him!"

And then—*crack!*—The door burst open. There she was. Our mom. Wild and beautiful and fierce, like a warrior queen straight out of a bedtime story I'd never been told. We sat on the floor, frozen in awe, as she swooped in, pulled us close, and whisked us away like it was the ending of some messy bullshit fairytale.

Uncle Roy was still yelling behind us, throwing curse words like a sailor. But she didn't flinch. "Fuck off!" she snapped, raising her hand as if she might slap him again for old time's sake. I'd never been so proud.

I didn't know where we were going, but I knew we'd been rescued. We took nothing with us. And that was enough. I kept praying after that. Not because I thought God finally picked up the phone, but because I knew He was listening.

The Cupcake That Meant Everything

School was not my strong suit. Though I excelled in math and wrote poetry that could impress kings, I couldn't function in front of others. I just tried to show up. Socializing felt like trying to speak fluent dolphin—everyone else seemed to get it, but I was just making weird noises and hoping for the best. Making friends was overwhelming, so I avoided it. When things got too intense, I bailed. I cut class, and eventually, I just stopped going back.

To make things even more complicated, I had an affliction. I found out I had endometriosis during a shift at my very first job, working at a fast-food place with other high schoolers who somehow had way more energy than anyone flipping burgers should. Out of nowhere, this tidal wave of pain hit me with sharp cramps, pressure, and nausea, like my insides were trying to fight their way out. I ended up on the floor, squirming around, breathing shallowly, trying to find *any* position that didn't feel like my organs were staging a mutiny.

The ambulance came and rushed me to the ER. After lots of poking, prodding, and medical jargon, the doctors finally told me I likely had endometriosis and needed to see a specialist.

Of course, when I got home, I didn't tell my dad the truth. I said it was just a stomach bug. I knew he wouldn't care, or worse, he'd try to "fix" it in the most unhelpful way possible. His priorities didn't really include things like doctor visits or emotional support. I tried my best to carry on.

But eventually, the weight of being sick and the endless responsibilities pressed down so hard that I couldn't focus anymore. I would sit in class, staring at the words on the page, and it was as if they slipped right through me. No matter how hard I tried, I couldn't hold on to a single thought long enough to make sense of it. So, I ran away from it all.

Exhaustion blurred everything—my mind, my body, even my will to be a good student. I made the hard decision to quit school, and when I did, it felt like no one noticed. No one asked why. The truth was, I couldn't explain it anyway.

After a couple of weeks of missing school, no one had any way to reach me. We didn't have cell phones, and our landline had been dead for who knows how long. Still, somehow, against all odds, my teacher found me. She found our little house tucked away at the end of that long dirt road.

One morning, I heard a loud horn honking in front of our fence.

It was Ms. Yelverton.

I recognized her voice immediately when the dogs started barking like crazy. But I didn't go outside. My dad did—probably thinking someone was there to call him out or get him in trouble. I stayed frozen in my bed, listening through the window, praying and panicking all at once. I didn't even get to see her. I just cried quietly, holding my breath as I heard her car pull away.

She had brought me a cupcake. Told my dad to wish me a happy birthday—something he hadn't remembered himself. That part stung more than I let on. She had gone so far out of her way to find me, probably with just an address, no GPS, just care and determination. And I couldn't even get out of bed to thank her.

That moment stuck with me, not just because she remembered my birthday when no one else did, but because I knew I had let her down. She had believed in me, cared enough to come looking, and I hid.

I never heard from her again. And maybe she thought I didn't care. Maybe she thought I didn't want her there. But the truth is... I just didn't know how to face kindness like that. Not when I felt so lost, so embarrassed by where I was and who I thought I had become.

If I could go back, I'd tell her thank you. I'd tell her that little act meant the world.

Even if I couldn't show it then.

All American Boy

Month after month, my affliction got the best of me. But one day, Eli came for me, my high school sweetheart, though we never really called it that. Around my dad, he played the part of just another one of my brother's friends. But between us, there was something unspoken, something that made me feel seen in a way I didn't understand yet.

He was the typical tall, dark, and handsome young man. He had a heart-stealing smile, with facial hair already in a five o'clock shadow after school. Grown women flirted with him everywhere, not knowing he was a teenager. His six-foot-two, muscular, athletic build made him a sight for sore eyes, and his deep voice only wanted to call me his.

He found me at the pond by the entrance of the school where we used to meet, barely able to stand, and didn't hesitate. He picked me up in his big, careful arms and carried me home, block after block, and up that long dirt road. We had to stop so many times because I was down in it from the pain. But he never rushed me. He just kept on truckin'.

Eli was everything someone would want their son to be. He was probably a junior at the time, a year and a half older than I. He had two parents who cared, and he was easily the most popular boy in school. He was undeniably likable and always cracking jokes. He had a smile as wide as the football field he played on. When he wasn't practicing throwing a pigskin, he was playing baseball and running track. He did it all. And he chose me.

I felt like nothing. Trash, really. I'll never understand why he cared so much, why he kept showing up for someone who was not even in the yearbook, someone who didn't even know how to receive love, let alone give it. I was rough around the edges. He didn't think so.

He pursued me, and all I did was push him away, afraid I would disappoint him. I wanted to shine for him. I wanted to be everything he thought I was. I didn't want to be the ragdoll meeting her prince charming. I wanted to be the princess. But I couldn't. I didn't have the means.

But that day, in his arms, I felt something unfamiliar, a kind of concern for me. And even if it didn't last, even if I didn't believe I deserved it, I'll never forget how it felt to be carried—not just physically, but emotionally, by someone who saw more in me than I saw in myself.

Life there was full of tough choices, hard decisions, and the only way I knew how to cope was to run and hide. I couldn't let myself fall into something so deep that I might not be able to keep the promises I thought I was supposed to make. I didn't trust that I could become the person I believed he wanted. I didn't think I'd ever fit in with his friends. The pressure was too much.

In my mind, he dreamed of someone soft and sweet, the kind of girl who wore her hair in ribbons and cheered on the sidelines, who came from a smiling family with dinners at six and picture-perfect holidays. I made up that girl in my head, the one who did everything right. And I was nothing like her.

But none of it was true. He loved me just as I was. He told everyone he did. His buddies and teammates would drive up the dirt road looking for him, always knowing he'd be right there with me. They teased him about it all the time, but he didn't care.

Even so, somewhere between what I feared and the life I was living, I couldn't believe I was ready for someone like him. It was heavy.

One day, Eli showed up not long after a fight I had with my dad. It wasn't just a shouting match. It was one of those dramatic fights where my dad always had to get the last word. My dad was drunk and furious about something I don't even remember now. I tried to stand my ground, yelling back as I ran to my room, "You're a drunk! "Go away!", but it didn't stop him.

He punched his fist through the flimsy wood of my bedroom door, making a hole the size of his big head. He threw a glass at me and missed, but it shattered all over the floor. I was afraid another beat-down was coming. I remember sitting on my mattress, holding up a pillow like it could somehow protect me, crying, terrified. The welts on my arms from last time had barely started to heal. He slurred more curses, threw my shit around, spat out hateful words, and then stormed off.

When Eli walked in with my brother and saw the wreckage a while later, the broken glass, the broken door, and me in tears, crying quietly, his whole face changed. He was furious. I could see it in his eyes. He wanted to charge down the hall and confront my dad, go toe to toe with him like some hero in a movie. But he didn't. He couldn't. He knew it would only make things worse, and he didn't have anywhere to take me. No safe place to escape to. And besides that, I didn't want Eli to get in any trouble. He had so much going for him. My battles weren't his.

He cautiously stepped into my room, crushing glass beneath his feet. My brother asked if I was okay, then shook his head and walked away as if defeated.

I feared my dad would hear Eli's big, heavy boots, but it couldn't get much worse at that point. I just really wanted a hug. Any more drama that could follow would be more than worth it if I collected just one hug from someone who truly cared for me.

"I love you," he whispered.

I wept quietly on his shoulder, wiping the mess on his coat, never saying those words back. He repeated it at least a dozen times, just like he always did. He rocked me back and forth as I cried. I wanted to believe it and let him love me.

He started to sing his favorite song, "Under the Bridge" by some grunge band that had just become popular at the time. Eli had an amazing voice, another one of his many talents. He sang that song every time we sat at the creek or took long walks, or just to cheer me up. I thought he was perfect.

But I knew I couldn't live the life he wanted to give me. Couldn't go to prom, couldn't go to homecoming, couldn't even afford a dress if by some miracle my dad had said yes. There were always chores waiting, yard work, housework, or just work. Dates were something that belonged in movies or someone else's life. I was stuck.

So, I told him to go. I told him that things would never change here. I knew he wouldn't walk away easily, so I told him I didn't love him. I wasn't sure if it was true; what I knew for certain was that I'd built walls so thick and high I didn't think love could get through. I was too ashamed to tell him the truth: that I didn't think I was good enough. That I didn't think *I* was enough.

My life was so hard, and this seemed easier than taking a risk only to be rejected later.

Sending him away didn't just break my heart—it broke my brothers' too. They looked up to Eli. He was everything we weren't used to. He was kind, funny, and normal. We were proud to have him around, even if just for a little while. He always pitched in with our chores. He would toss his shirt and start the lawnmower. He would practice sports with my brothers. He was the hero we didn't know we needed.

And I think I broke Eli that day, too. He was bright, somewhere in between a man and a boy, still learning how to solve all of life's problems.

But not mine.

Living with my parents was like hopping from one sinking boat to another, and no one, not even Eli, could reach us.

But deep down, I believed it was the right thing. Eli would have done anything for me. Anything. And that was a problem. Life there was a dumpster fire. I had to let him go, or he would go up in smoke with us.

I saw him wipe a tear with his sleeve. "I don't believe you," he said as he stared at me with eyes hoping I would change my mind.

Eventually, when all was said and done, he left quietly out the back door. Never to return.

My older brother claimed to have seen him a few years after high school; he was hanging with the wrong crowds now, no longer playing sports. He said he looked tired. Then he said, "Oh, yeah, Eli told me to tell you he still loves you". I thought it was sad.

Years later, I saw him again as well. I was walking through the city. He looked so different, so grown, with a beard, surrounded by friends. I didn't recognize him at first. Then I heard it.

"Hey, you!" he called out.

That voice. So familiar it stopped me cold. I turned around and smiled.
"Eli?"

"Yeah, it's me!" he said, with that smile I could hear. And before I knew it, he pulled me into a hug that lifted me right off the ground. For a second, it felt like high school again. Like my tiny self, floating in his big arms all over again.

He set me down and, in true Eli fashion, shouted, "I still love you, girl!"

I wanted to tell him I was sorry. I wanted to be forgiven. I wanted to explain so much, but I couldn't. I moved on. I didn't want to rehash anything. I didn't know him anymore.

"Eli, you look happy," I said, laughing nervously.

I patted his chest, a quiet farewell in itself, my hand brushing the familiar steel-hard strength that once held me close. I could feel he wanted to linger, to talk, maybe even turn back time for just a moment

But I couldn't. I couldn't go back.

"Take care of yourself," I said, my voice slightly cracking, as I turned and walked away, slowly exhaling as if letting him go unwillingly all over again. I could feel him watching me, maybe even hoping I'd turn back around.

I forced a smile as I walked away, holding it all close. But I knew he was okay now, and that was enough.

I'm Not Coming Out of This Closet

What the hell was I even thinking? Likely only thirteen or fourteen, one episode of another shelter stay landed me in the care of a county social worker. This was part of the long list of people I felt I had let down as a kid in a system that was failing me instead.

She was tall and a little chubby, with a round face and rosy cheeks. Her short, grey-blonde hair framed a kind smile behind her glasses. Her voice was the calmest I'd ever heard. She had a warmth about her that made you feel safe without even trying. My older brother let her in, and as she made her way to the back room where I slept, all I could feel was the weight of embarrassment of letting someone so kind see the mess of the place I called home.

She tried her best to see me in that tiny closet. I stood there pretending to look for something, though I had no idea what or why I was even hiding. I just knew I was ashamed. Ashamed of the house we lived in, of my dad, of the plain, undecorated room that felt nothing like a girl's space, and of the clothes I had on, worn, mismatched, and ugly in my eyes.

I was like a toddler squeezing my eyes shut, hoping the world would disappear. I sat on a box of clothes, tucked into the shadows, while she sat gently on my mattress, barely able to see me. I answered her questions in a whisper, my voice small and careful, as she gently coaxed me to come out. She didn't push.

And by the next visit, she came with a new approach—one that worked better.

"What's this dog's name?" she asked, motioning to our shaggy grey dog. "That's Tooney," I replied.

Tooney was a lovebug, friendly with everyone. He'd followed me home one night after I ran away, and because he wouldn't stop trailing behind me, I felt like I had no choice but to go back home with him. Looking back, he probably saved me that night. But I think I saved him, too.

"Would you like to take Tooney to the park and get some Cokes?" she offered.

We got into her car, Tooney and me, and ended up at a park with a wide stretch of grass. He chased butterflies like something out of a movie, running wild and happy. I don't remember what we talked about, but I remember how I felt. For the first time in a long time, I felt happy around an adult. Really happy.

I wish there had been more visits like that. She could have been the one to save me. She might've helped me find a way out of the madness I lived in. There was so much potential in that moment, so much quiet hope. I didn't want her to leave me. I wanted a way out. I imagined all the ways I could show her I trusted her. I wanted a better life.

But when she gently asked if I was okay, if I was safe, I lied. I said yes. I was too ashamed to admit the truth. And I never saw her again.

The Most Unhappy Place

I remember the sound of my mama's voice behind the closed bedroom door, sharp, clipped, repeating *no* over and over, until it bled into cursing. Then the door flew open, and there was my dad, back without missing a beat. He crouched down, grinning, and asked if I wanted to go to this amazing theme park—where the big mouse lived, where all the princesses waited, where dreams came true—with my aunts and cousins.

Of course, I wanted to go. I had only ever dreamed of it. I jumped up and down, my little body unable to hold still, and ran to grab my clothes.

By the time the day arrived, my dad had packed all my things neatly into a large, round, green duffel bag. He drove me to my grandparents' house, where the look on their faces told me I was not exactly welcome.

My dad had a way of trading favors with his family. Through his job, he got discounted airline tickets to anywhere in the world, and in exchange, his relatives would do things for him, like add me to their weekend plans when they didn't really want to.

"Load up," my grandfather ordered, pointing toward the big van in the driveway. It seated at least ten of us. I climbed into the second row, excited, but my teenage aunts shifted away from me, muttering in their language for him to make me move. He grabbed my arm, pulled me down the narrow aisle, and sent me to the back row.

Still, my excitement didn't waver. The drive was long, about six hours, maybe more, with pit stops at gas stations that smelled of dust and burnt coffee. But none of that mattered. I was on my way.

When we finally pulled up to my dad's older sister, Alene's, house, she opened the door and gathered everyone in a hug. Everyone but me. I watched as my younger aunts explained to her why I was there, their voices low, their eyes sliding in my direction.

But I didn't let it sink in. I kept my focus on the dream. The park. The castle. The mouse. The princesses.

For the first time in my life, the thing I had only ever imagined, so much happiness, was just around the corner.

We stayed the night at my aunt and uncle's house before visiting the park. It was a big house out in the country, with half a dozen rooms. At least three of them sat empty, waiting. My younger aunts and cousins ran down the hall squealing, claiming each one like a prize. I tried to follow, but before I could step inside, they darted out and told their mothers that I was there, like my presence was something to report.

A moment later, my aunt appeared. Her voice was flat, final: *"You can have the couch."*

I didn't argue with adults. I never did.

Back then, I brushed it off, the way I brushed off so many little cruelties. I told myself maybe I was being annoying. Maybe I *was* the problem. That seemed to be the case everywhere I went. It was easier to believe that than to admit the truth—that they simply didn't want me.

By nightfall, every bedroom was filled. Laughter and whispers drifted down the hallway, muffled behind closed doors. Two of the girls ended up having to share the living room with me, their faces twisted with irritation at being stuck there.

I told myself not to care. And lying on that pull-out bed, listening to everyone mingle, felt odd. But I was too exhausted from the drive to let it bother me.

Sometime in the middle of the night, long after I had drifted into a deep sleep on the couch sofa bed, I felt myself being lifted. I opened my eyes just enough to see my aunt carrying me down the hall. Still half-dreaming, I relaxed into her arms—until I realized where we were. She set me down on the carpeted floor of a boy's bedroom. My cousin was already asleep in the bed a few feet away.

She dropped a thin blanket beside me and spoke sharply, her words cutting through the dark: *"You have lice, so we had to move you here."* Then she slammed the door.

I sat there stunned, still groggy from sleep, my heart pounding. Lice?

I knew what it was—everyone did. But I had never had it. The school nurse checked our hair often, and mine was always clear. My neighbor Annie used to braid my hair almost every day; she would have said something if she'd seen even the smallest trace.

But none of that mattered in that moment. What mattered was the shame. The confusion. The way her voice made it sound like I was dirty, contagious, something to be moved out of sight.

I pulled the blanket over me and lay there on the hard floor, wide awake now, too stunned to cry, too confused to sleep.

I tried to get comfortable on that floor and just stared up into the dark. Memories crept in—the way my grandparents and aunts used to treat me when I lived with them for that short, bitter stretch of time. The sharp words, the cold looks, the way I always seemed to be in the way. The weight of it pressed down on me, and before I knew it, I was crying. But I didn't dare let anyone hear. That was the night I learned how to cry silently, swallowing every sob so it wouldn't escape.

From the corner of my eye, I saw my cousin peering down at me from his small bed. I remembered how they treated him, too, the way he was made into a punching bag for the same family that bruised me. But he was smiling. Maybe he was just happy not to be alone.

So, I smiled back, a fragile, tired smile. And then, finally, I let myself fall asleep.

By morning, the heaviness had lifted. The park was waiting, and I ran through it wide-eyed, dizzy with excitement. For a while, I almost forgot about the night before. Almost.

Once we stepped into the park, my grandmother announced that everyone should use the bathrooms first. That's when the misery began.

My teenage aunt—the one who was always bitching about something—suddenly lifted her sleeve and showed a faint red mark on her arm. She turned to my older aunt and said, loud enough for everyone to hear, *"Look what she did to me! She gave me a rash. She was leaning on me last night."*

My stomach dropped. I shook my head "no" quickly, silently pleading with my aunt to believe me, to see that it wasn't true. She nodded as if she didn't believe me and told us to hurry on.

But when we got inside the tiled echo of the bathroom, my younger aunt yanked me by the arm, her face twisted with rage. *"You fucking bitch,"* she hissed, venom dripping from every word. *"I hope you get lost in the park."*

I stumbled into the nearest stall, my hands shaking, heart thundering in my chest. I sat on the toilet, holding my breath, listening as their voices carried through the room. They were mocking me, tearing me apart. All I could think was: *please don't leave me here. Please still be outside when I'm done.*

When I finally stepped out, I washed my hands quickly, afraid to even look up. But in the mirror's reflection, I caught sight of them shuffling out the door without me.

I ran from the sinks, water dripping from my fingers, and then bolted out into the daylight. My eyes scanned the crowds, frantic. They were gone.

I spotted my grandfather a few yards away, sitting on a bench in the distance. Relief washed over me as I ran to him, desperate for someone—anyone—to anchor me. I asked where everyone had gone.

He didn't even look concerned. He just patted my head and, with that thick, jagged accent that always made his words harder to understand, said almost cheerfully, *"Nobody wanna play with you."* My mouth wanted to smile with him, but my eyes wanted to cry.

There was nothing funny about it. His eyes were empty, his voice hollow. It was like he didn't have a soul. It was like none of these fucking people had souls.

I stood there, confused, my small body filled with shame. My eyes darted around, searching for a phone booth, an adult, or some way to call my dad to come rescue me. My grandfather was right there, but somehow, I was still lost.

I turned and watched the park move around me as if I wasn't even part of it. Children were shrieking with joy on spinning carousels, families laughing, and rides swinging back and forth. Their happiness only made the truth sink in deeper: I wasn't going to be a part of that magic. Not today. Not ever.

Then my grandmother appeared, trailed by my aunt Alene's husband—a man I had never even met. She told me flatly that he would "watch me today." I stared at him, a stranger, and then back at her, but she was already turning away. He didn't look like a picker or a farmer. He made me nervous. She mumbled something in her language to my grandfather. He turned around and shoved a couple of crumpled dollars into my hand and muttered, *"Go get ice cream."*

And then, just like that, they walked away into the castle. I stood outside, clutching a few crumpled dollars, watching their backs disappear through the stone arches. The castle was the kind of place supposed to be full of magic. But for me, it was a reminder of what couldn't be.

My uncle by marriage, Dwayne, was a tall, dorky man with thick glasses and a mustache. I didn't feel safe with him, though I couldn't explain why. His questions made me shrink further into myself—*Are you shy? What did you do to get in trouble? How did you make them mad? Why didn't your parents come?* I had no answers. I hadn't done anything wrong. I just wanted to have fun. But by then, I only felt regret.

He said we'd ride the ferry around the park and see if we spot any of my aunts. I nodded. I had no choice. What else could I do? I almost kept my eyes on the ground the whole time, refusing to look at the laughter and colors swirling around me. I didn't want to see joy when it wasn't mine. As we walked toward the boats, I kept looking back one last time at the rides, desperate not to drift so far from the fun I had longed for.

But that was it. Just like always, the gestures of kindness were taken away, carried off by people who seemed to take pleasure in pulling them from me.

We rode the ferry, and he pointed out things as we sped past. I still wanted to look. A sliver of hope fluttered inside me—I wanted to have fun. I was just a little girl.

When the ride finally ended, I got an ice cream, and we sat on a bench. It dripped onto my shirt. He handed me a napkin and asked if my grandmother would be upset. Probably knew her better than I did. She was the kind of person to yell, *"Off with your head!"* at the slightest mistake.

At some point, everyone rounded up, and we trudged back to the van. They all insisted I sit alone—reasons piled up like excuses: lice, rashes, chocolate ice cream stains. I even heard my youngest aunt mutter, *"It's probably shit."* Terrible adults raising terrible children.

Arriving back at Alene's house should have felt like relief. It didn't. My sweet cousin, the one I shared a room with, made a silly joke that his mom didn't like. She grabbed a large shoe and beat him over the head, again and again. He raised his arms to block her, but she kept hitting, even after dropping the shoe. He was laughing, likely just trying to piss her off, but I could see the tears beneath his arms.

I quietly snuck back into our room before the sun even went down, and I curled up on the floor with my pillow. I never understood why they treated him that way. Every time I saw my cousin, he had scars and bruises. He ran into the room shortly after me and sat on his bed, staring down at me as we both held back

47

tears. It was as if we recognized something about each other, two kids, like something from Never-Neverland, that nobody ever wanted.

"It didn't even hurt anyway," he mumbled, throwing himself back on the bed and staring at the ceiling.

I don't remember the ride home. I just tried to sleep through it, to tune all of them out. My cousin lived near the park, so he wasn't on the trip with us home, but I thought about him the whole time.

When they dropped me off at home, pretending that I had a great time, something shifted inside me that felt heavy, weary, and unfamiliar. My grandparents walked me up to the door where my dad waited. I bypassed him and made a beeline for my Mama, who was waiting inside.

Mama stood in the hall, ready to greet me. I dropped my bag and leapt into her arms, wrapping my legs around her and crying uncontrollably.

"What?" she asked, startled.

I didn't know the words, not really. But I let it all come out: "It was the worst time of my life. I hate them all."

I told her everything about how awful they were, the things they said, how they beat my cousin, how they sent me away with Dwayne. I sobbed between words, losing control, letting it all out. I had never been happier to be home in our tiny apartment than in that moment.

And Mama was fuming. My dad walked in, and she filled him in. Now we were both crying. My dad kneeled down and asked me some questions that I tried to answer through tears.

Before I could finish, he snatched his keys, stormed out the door, fired up his motorcycle, and said, "Heads are gonna roll."

The Almost Fairytale

Mama was down on her luck again. Truth be told, I don't think she ever had it easy. Not yet old enough to order a drink, she was already raising two toddlers. She didn't have a license, but she knew how to drive, and that was enough. Every so often, someone would hand her the keys to a tired old car, a gift meant to help us get to appointments or just around town. They were lemons, every one of them, but Mama always found a way to make them run.

One night, we were headed home in one of those beat-up cars. Mama was grinning and listening to the radio, proud to have wheels under us, no matter the age or condition. As long as it moved, she was grateful. Then—BANG. A sharp pop cut through the night, and the car jerked, swaying hard left and right. Mama gasped but kept her hands steady. She shouted once, but her voice never cracked. She never lost control.

When she eased us onto the narrow shoulder of that pitch-black road, she turned with a sheepish smile and apologized, over and over. We sat wide-eyed and rattled, but Mama stayed calm.

"Don't worry, we're okay," she said, soothing us with her steady voice, as if it were the only thing keeping the night from swallowing us whole.

Then came a terrible sound, it was a man's cry, raw and ragged, cutting through the dark as Mama opened the car door.

A homeless man had been struck in the leg by the hubcap, flung loose when our tire blew. I didn't really understand what had happened, only that our wheel was bare and the man was hurt.

Mama rushed toward him, her voice rambling out apologies. She tried to calm him, begged him to stay still so she could call for help. But he was furious, drunk, cursing, and swatting her away.

Another man appeared out of the shadows, laid a steadying hand on his friend, and turned to Mama with quiet thanks before helping him limp off into the night.

Mama was frustrated.

She stood there in the silence they left behind, confusion written across her face. I remember thinking how unfair it all was, that she could try so hard to make things right, and still end up blamed, rejected, or pushed aside. Even then, I think I understood that life never gave her the luxury of being just a mother. She was always putting out fires, smoothing over crises, carrying the weight of mistakes that weren't always hers.

Mama looked into the car at us and told us to get out. My brother's voice piped up with questions, sounding more frightened, but she didn't have time for answers. She took us each by the hand and led us down the dark road until we reached a pay phone. I don't remember how long we waited there, or even what she planned to do, but eventually a set of headlights cut through the night. A big tow truck rumbled toward us like some kind of savior.

It was Tim.

Tim was our neighbor back at the apartment complex, not much older than Mama. I think he stayed in apartment 2 with his grandfather, whom he looked after. I hadn't paid him much mind before. Sometimes he would stop to talk to Mama when we were playing on the grass, but to me, he was just another grown-up in the background.

That night, though, he looked like a superhero. He was tall, broad, protective. The kind of person you somehow knew would step in if you needed back-up.

Funny thing is, Mama had that same quality. She could be tough, fierce even, when she thought someone needed help. I remember one afternoon, my brother and I were sitting on the patchy grass outside our building while Mama kept watch nearby. Tim's grandfather was shuffling across the street, tapping the curb with his cane. Mama sprang into action; certain he was struggling. She shouted for us to stay put and rushed over.

But instead of gratitude, he shoved her away and snapped at her, his voice sharp with pride or anger. I couldn't tell which. Mama froze, threw her hands up, and walked back to us; her face caught between embarrassment and disbelief.

"He's not stuck, he's collecting walnuts from the ground," she said as she laughed it off.

Up above him stood a tall walnut tree, and the sidewalk was littered with shells.

When Tim's tow truck pulled up, my brother and I glanced at each other with awe. The thing was massive, with blinding lights and an engine that growled like a monster in the night. Relief washed over us. Tim stepped down, quiet as always, but beneath his thick mustache was a smile meant just for us. We knew he drove a tow truck, but never once imagined we'd be the ones needing it. That night, it wasn't just a truck or a service. To us, it was a kindness we'd been aching for, and our hearts were full of excitement as we climbed up in the cab.

After that night, I couldn't stop thinking about Tim. I found myself waiting for glimpses of him and watching from the grass as he came and went from his apartment. He always looked the same, wearing a dark green heavy coat, jeans, sturdy work boots, and hair neatly combed as he closed the heavy wooden door behind him. In my child's heart, I secretly hoped he would fall in love with Mama and keep showing up as our hero.

In those moments of daydreaming, I forgot about my father, the man who had left us, the man who had left scars. I didn't question his absence anymore. Tim became the figure I wanted to fill that space. He seemed like someone strong, steady, and safe. I longed for him to be in our lives somehow, as a friend, a protector, maybe even family.

But Mama didn't see him the way I did. To her, whatever was between them was nothing more than neighborly. I didn't understand it then. She admitted once that he scared her a little, that she'd seen him in a fistfight outside the building one night. She said he was a tough guy. I think she was also guarding herself from another man who might bring chaos.

So, she left it at that. And she squashed the fairytale I had built in my head. As a child, I couldn't understand why she wouldn't reach for someone who looked like safety to me. As an adult, I know she had already lived enough disappointment to recognize what danger might look like dressed as strength.

A Pack of Wolves

Both of my parents came from families of eleven children each, and somehow, that made us poorer in love rather than richer. I used to think the bigger the family, the more laughter, the more shoulders to lean on, but in ours, it was the opposite. It was like the smaller the family, the stronger they stood, and the larger, the more they crumbled under their own weight.

    My grandparents had been pickers, bent over fields to make ends meet, but I don't think they ever wanted that kind of life for their children. Still, they had child after child, until there were too many to keep track of.

    What boggled my mind most was how, out of so many aunts and uncles, hardly any seemed capable of being a decent human. Some numbed themselves with addiction, others chased danger or disappeared into the military, and the rest carried grudges like trophies.

    Instead of pulling together, they split into cliques, each side of the family with its own petty alliances. The women bickered and excluded each other like high school rivals, while the men ganged up on each other, their tempers spilling into drunken fistfights.

    My aunts were the worst. They spent hours getting ready for the clubs, hairspray can after hairspray can, acting like they were better than everyone. They weren't shit.

The cousins weren't much different. Most aunts and uncles had children, but instead of big family gatherings, there were scattered little circles, one sibling hosting, while another wasn't invited. If someone "married up," they suddenly became selective about who still counted as family. My dad, especially, was often left out. His own brothers-in-law excluded him without shame, and we followed his shadow into that loneliness.

It was a hellish family to be born into. Both sides. All I ever wanted was to feel like I belonged somewhere in that sea of names. When life got hard, I would sit with a bitter question: how could I have twenty aunts and uncles, dozens of cousins, and still rarely ever have a single person to call for a ride, a few dollars, or even someone to cheer me on at a dance recital? They felt less like family and more like strangers who happened to share my blood.

Over the years, I tried to reach out to show them I was a good kid, that I was worth their attention. Sometimes, an aunt would give me a little of her time, a brief flicker of connection. But it was never consistent. No clique ever opened its doors to me.

So, I quietly wrote them off, carrying with me the ache of wanting a family that felt like more than just a shitty pack of wolves.

Poor and Poorer

Marty wasn't the only boy in the area. The sticks seemed to collect "lost boys," and somehow, most of them ended up at our house.

Curtis was one of them. He had this restless, jumpy energy that earned him the nickname "Jungle Boy." He lived with his grandmother in a nearby mobile home, not far from Marty. The two of them never really clicked—Marty barely tolerated him—but in that lost part of the city, we were all thrown together whether we wanted to be or not.

Curtis was closer to Marty's age, but already carrying the weight of adult mistakes. A high school dropout, a young father, always smelled of pot. People in town complained about him often, and more than once, we saw the police come to haul him off.

Then one day, Curtis showed up, saying his grandmother had kicked him out and taken his keys. He wasn't welcome at his kid's mother's place either, which left him with nowhere to go. Curtis wasn't the type to crash on couches like some of the other boys. He always carried a wad of cash in his pocket, always had some odd job going. He even made fun of the ones who drifted between our couches, though sometimes he dragged them along to work for extra help.

But outside of that hustle, he didn't have much. And neither did we. My dad worked odd shifts and usually didn't get home until three in the morning. My brothers and I would stay up waiting, hoping he'd bring back airplane food from his job, because if we didn't wait, we didn't eat.

Curtis asked my older brother if he could crash for a night or two, just until he got his keys back, so he could grab his car and move on. My brother hesitated. He didn't know Curtis *that* well, and Marty's side-eye wasn't helping. But Curtis wouldn't let up. He sweetened the deal: if we let him stay, he'd break into his grandmother's kitchen, steal all the groceries he'd just bought, and cook us dinner and breakfast.

Marty burst out laughing, pointing out how packed our house already was. James and Aaron had been camped out on the floor and couch for weeks, and when Marty and my brother worked late at the landfill, Marty would end up crashing there, too. "It's too risky, she'll call the cops," he said.

But Curtis wasn't deterred. "It's my food!" he kept saying for justification.

Somehow, my brother was sold. "Alright," he said, grinning. "Let's do this before Dad gets home."

"Jungle Boy" practically bounced off the walls, high-fiving everyone like he'd just hit the jackpot, and led the charge toward the backyard fence. My brother assigned me to look out while Curtis hoisted himself through the kitchen window. Marty gave him a boost, and the next thing we heard was a heavy *thud* from inside.

We all doubled over, choking back laughter, trying to keep quiet. It was ridiculous, and we knew it—but that was Curtis.

Jungle Boy peeked out the window, put a finger to his lips to hush us, then grinned so wide, whispering loudly, "Just think of all the chicken and sausages we're gonna get!" His eyes gleamed like he had just broken into a bank.

My brother rubbed his hands together, already tasting the loot. Marty, though, shook his head and muttered on repeat, "He's gonna get caught, he's gonna get caught…" like a broken record.

Meanwhile, Curtis started passing food through the window like he was running a drive-thru. He tossed some to Marty, some to my brother, some to Aaron, and some to James. First came the chicken, then the pack of hot dogs, then some pork chops. He even threw in some boxed mashed potatoes and gravy, like it was Christmas morning. I carried a jug of sweet tea. When our arms were full, he just tossed the extra stuff onto the grass. Marty gave him a lift back out the window, and the lot of us tore through the yard, hopping fences in the dark like we were a gang of wild raccoons.

Curtis never stopped laughing, high-pitched, breathless, practically cheering for himself the whole way. "Woo-hoo!" he kept yelling, like a little kid getting away with swiping candy instead of stealing food.

We jumped over sticks and rocks, trying to hustle through the endless brush in the backyard. James even dropped the pack of hot dogs, which my dogs devoured immediately. He was always the clumsy one, "Damn it!" I heard him yell as he kept on running.

By the time we staggered back inside, arms full of half-frozen treasure, we realized too late that the clock had turned against us. Dad would be rolling up in less than thirty minutes. We loaded everything onto the table. The whole place was flickering in the weak glow of kerosene lamps because the power was out again. Jungle Boy looked satisfied. My brother nervously tried to talk him out of cooking, afraid of what my dad would say, and rightfully so.

The meat was still as solid as bricks, but Curtis wasn't fazed. He just lit the gas stove with his lighter, clanged a pan down, and started opening up the pork chops. The whole thing was wild. He looked like a ghost tearing apart our kitchen on a haunted movie set.

"It's too dark, let's just wait for the morning," my brother said.

"Nah, I'll just make it romantic with the candles," Curtis joked.

It felt less like dinner and more like a shit-show was about to go down, but Curtis was grinning ear to ear, proud as hell, as if he'd just saved the day instead of ransacking his grandma's freezer.

As expected, my dad came home, but was empty-handed this time. He noticed Curtis right away and sharply asked, "What are you doing here, Jungle Boy?"

Curtis straightened his back, turned on his "respectable voice," and politely gave him a rundown of the situation. For a second, it almost sounded reasonable. But my dad wasn't a man of reason.

Without missing a beat, my dad marched over, slammed the knob on the stove to *off*, and barked, "You can stay, but everyone needs to go to bed right now. I'm tired. I'm not sleeping with pots and pans banging around."

We pleaded with him, but that was like trying to negotiate with a brick wall. He snapped at us, "If y'all don't shut the fuck up, I am throwing all this fucking food out!"

Then, to prove his point, he grabbed the tube of chorizo and launched it out the door like it owed him money before blowing out the kerosene lamps. It was like he snuffed out not just the lights but every ounce of hope we had for a midnight feast.

Curtis broke into laughter watching the chorizo fly away, but still hollered, "No! Not the sausage!"

We sulked in silence, stomachs growling, hopes dashed. My brother muttered, "You can take it back if you want."

"Hell no," Curtis grinned, shaking his head. "Let's start the grill."

That was Curtis in a nutshell: broke as the rest of us, but too stubborn to admit it. He always managed to dress his poverty up in swagger, like duct tape sprayed gold. And somehow, God kept tossing us all together—poor, hungry kids convincing ourselves we could turn things around, and that night, we actually did.

Freakshow Attractions

Summer came, and I missed my mama, even though I was ashamed to admit it. I spent too many days piecing her together through the scraps of stories my brothers and grandmother told, trying to convince myself she'd come back. That she hadn't forgotten me.

But the truth was, she *hadn't* forgotten. She just didn't want to come back. She chose to leave me behind. When she ran, she didn't flinch, didn't hesitate, didn't even look over her shoulder. No second thoughts. No regret. That's what separated us—she was hardened, cold in all the ways I wasn't. When it came time to choose, she always chose herself. I wasn't even an afterthought to her.

I felt frustrated with my life, so I did what any irrational teenager would do in my shoes. I joined the carnival.

My grandmother used to tell me stories about our family, the gypsies, travelers, and artisans who moved from farm to farm, dancing with castanets and singing for their keep. There was something beautiful in that freedom, that creativity, so I decided to carry a piece of that spirit forward, in my own way. The carnival felt like the perfect place. It was somewhere I could belong without having to explain myself. A place that welcomed me as I was, yet gave me the space to figure things out. But the fair was anything but fair.

After I got in, lo and behold, my mama was there. I felt indifferent. This was *my* escape. My shot at something different. I wasn't chasing dreams anymore. I was letting them go. I was trying to accept the life I was born into, and make peace with surviving as the kind of person the world already assumed I was. The "trash" they expected me to be.

I never believed there was space for me in the kind of life Aunt Cathy had, the clean, happy home. That felt like another universe. At the time, I couldn't imagine a future where someone like me, raised by addicts, could ever break out and become something better. Not where we came from. Not in our neighborhood. I was a *carnie* now.

But there she was working the carnival games and hustling money in her usual scandalous way. She lied, she stole, and got caught more than once when her numbers didn't match what she was selling. They kept moving her to different booths just to keep an eye on her. She didn't care.

And I was so desperate to reconnect with her, to maybe fix something between us, that I tried stealing too—five bucks here, ten bucks there. But I had a conscience I couldn't quiet, no matter how hard I tried. I didn't want to disappoint anyone, or worse, get kicked out of the only place I'd ever felt like I might belong, among other misfits like me. So, I stopped cheating.

I wasn't like her.

Carnies were a weird bunch, and everyone knew it. I was surrounded by the strangest mix of people you could imagine. There was "Bubba" the clown, and even Elvis hollering and whistling for young couples to bite the bait.

Homeboys, jocks, goody two-shoes, even girls my age would wander up and ask, "How the hell did *you* end up working in the booths?" like I was some tragic mystery. I could see it in their faces, this beautiful, sweet, teenage girl, hiding behind a shy smile and rough attitude, stuck in what they all saw as life's last resort.

Little did they know, I would have given anything to be on their side of the booths, holding hands with someone or laughing vivaciously with friends holding stuffed bears.

Then came the local sheriff. For some reason, he took a shine to me. And yeah, maybe I *should've* lied about my age, but I didn't. I told him I was a minor, but that my mom worked with me. I figured honesty would keep things simple. I was naïve. I thought if I was friendly enough, maybe he'd go easy on her if she got caught stealing again.

But night after night, he kept coming around, always with some half-baked excuse, asking about fights, thefts, whatever drama popped up. But it was all bullshit. Even if I *had* known anything, I wasn't saying a word. He didn't care about the carnival drama. What he saw was a lost, pretty, peasant girl, and he wanted to play the hero. I wasn't buying it.

He was probably in his thirties and had been a cop long enough to think he could get away with anything. He wore a Stetson like he was in some bad Western, had a thick mustache, and slicked-back hair when he wasn't wearing that damn hat. Tall, but not exactly fit—just big enough to think he was intimidating.

At first, he tried to play it cool, asking if I was into any of the "stuff" some of the other carnie girls were doing. I didn't know what he meant until he spelled it out. Drugs. Prostitution. Apparently, that was happening right under my nose, but I had my own problems.

Then he straight-up asked me out. I was shocked. He knew I was a minor. He knew my mom was working nearby. And still, he told me to meet him after closing. Like it was nothing. Like I'd be flattered. What the hell was he thinking? I knew things were tough, but I was still just a kid.

I knew right away I wasn't going anywhere with that man, but I played it off like I might. I smiled, nodded, and gave him just enough to keep him from getting pissed. Guys like that, entitled and full of power, can get really butt-hurt if you bruise their ego. I played my hand safe.

He gave me instructions like it was a mission: meet him at the 7-Eleven down the block, before midnight. He said he'd be on his motorcycle, wearing a black jacket and a red helmet. Really dramatic.

As we closed up and turned in our cash, I told my mom what happened. She just rolled her eyes and said,

"You really gonna go hang out with some old-ass cop?"

Hell no. Never. The thought grossed me out. No matter how much I wanted to run again, this wasn't it. This wasn't the train I was gonna take.

We both hitched a ride with my brother's friend to get food afterward. As we drove past the store, we saw the sheriff standing out there in the parking lot next to his bike, looking cautiously out towards the street.

"There goes your friend," she said.

I glanced over my shoulder one more time and could see the carnival lights flickering faintly like memories in a rearview. Why did he want to see me that night? I'll never know. But I felt a sense of pride, for just a second, being just like my mother, playing with someone's mind just before running and burning that bridge to the ground. I knew I couldn't go back.

And just like that, it was the final thread tying me to a world of sawdust, laughter, and illusion. I left it all behind with only the clothes on my back and a few dollars in my bag.

A Lonely Place Without You

For years, I read my dad's postcards from Texas until the ink was faded and barely visible. Each one was a little piece of a better world, the world he came from. They showcased pictures of crimson sunsets bleeding across the sky, fields of bluebonnets and yellow roses, dusty roads, lonely highways, and old pick-up trucks like the ones he always drove. On the cover of my favorite card, it read, "Texas is a lonely place without you…"

My dad's whole family came from or still lives in Texas, and he visited often. They left footprints everywhere, from Brownsville to Amarillo, with memories tucked into little small towns in between. Every time he packed his bags, I begged him to take me back to the world I was so desperate to be a part of. It was the only place I could imagine being happy. I loved Texas. I loved the people and the barbecue. I loved the flat lands and the thunderstorms. I loved his accent. And his cousins were local heroes, winning the county fair's fajita contest more times than anyone could count. In my young heart, Texas wasn't a destination. It was home.

It was a cool, brisk evening when I headed out to use the payphone that stood by itself at the corner of the block, about half a mile from our house. I tried twice to reach my cousin, Valerie, but no one answered. Val and I were close, but she was promiscuous. I was shy and reserved. Val was always up for an adventure. We would chat on the phone until my coins ran out, planning our next good time.

I hung up the phone after the tenth ring went unanswered, collected my refund, and that's when I saw him. He was tall. He was different. He was Rick.

Rick walked by slowly, locking eyes with me as if we'd both seen an apparition of some sort. We never met prior to this encounter, but I instantly recognized his swagger. He was wearing a worn brown flannel jacket over a plain white tee, blue jeans falling over scuffed, mud-caked boots. His hair was short but a little wild, with soft waves that just barely grazed his deep brown eyes.

There was something in the way he carried himself, casual, like he belonged anywhere. It was curious. And yet, all I could think was: *Where did this guy come from?*

I watched him walk away as he headed toward the corner store. I stayed at the payphone, frozen, the receiver still in my hand, but the dial tone long gone. Minutes passed. The idea of going back to that dark, cold house with no phone, no heat, no one, settled in my chest like a weight. I didn't want to go back. But I didn't know what else to do.

Then, behind me, a gentle voice broke through the silence.

"Hello there."

I gripped the phone tightly, unsure if I imagined it. I turned slowly, and there he was again. He was standing just a few feet away, flipping a box of Camel cigarettes in his hand, packing them with that steady up-and-down motion.

I didn't know what to say. My mind was spinning. I didn't talk to the boys. Eli was gone. I had no business making friends with the way my life was. I was overthinking in a matter of seconds. I looked over at him.

He looked at me and offered his hand, casual and warm, like we'd known each other in another life.

"I'm Rick," he said.

He was charming, with manners unheard of in this part of town. He was relaxed when he spoke. I was smitten, but not by his looks or his charm. I knew deep inside me he was Texan. I just knew it. It was like a dream. I couldn't go to Texas, so Texas came to me.

What started as small talk turned into long, meandering walks that stretched across several weeks. We wandered through quiet streets and dusty paths, trading stories like secrets. Rick was born and raised in McAllen, Texas, a town with heat that clung to your skin and skies that stretched wide and endless. He was only here for a while, tagging along with his best friend Max, who had family in town. Like me, Rick was looking for an escape from the noise and mess of whatever waited for him back home.

Before long, I knew he liked me. It was there in the way he listened when I spoke, in the way his eyes lingered just a second longer than they needed to. It was how he let me lean my head on his shoulder when we watched the stars. How he'd sketch pictures of me at the park that made me look beautiful. But he never said it out loud. Never tried to kiss me. He never held my hand long enough to make me think it was more. Still, from the night we met, we became inseparable. Rick was quiet, steady, and unforgettable.

But as quickly as this spark ignited, it also faded away. Rick had to return to McAllen with Max. Our long, deep conversations slowly dwindled. Everything we talked or laughed about echoed away in the night, never to be heard again. Our brief friendship started feeling like abandonment, and he knew it, too. I was young and hopeful, and I realized that sometimes, no matter how close someone feels to your heart, they can still leave you behind.

I was learning, painfully and quietly, what it meant to want someone to stay, if that's what it was... and to be left anyway.

I Never Made it to McAllen, Texas

For months, Rick and I traded letters through good old-fashioned snail mail. It took me ten minutes to walk to the end of the dusty dirt road and check the mailbox, but it became my favorite ritual. Sure, email existed, and so did the phone and pagers, but I didn't have access to any of that. All I had were stamps I helped myself to from my dad's collection, pieced together from unclaimed property at his job. I had no clue how much they were worth to a collector, and honestly, I didn't give two shits. To me, they were priceless. His letters carried the words of the one person who could make me smile, folded into envelopes that felt like hope.

Rick told me he and Max would be coming back for the summer, though not for as long as the last time. Still, I held onto that. I spent months wondering if I'd actually see him again, or if he'd just fade into memory.

They were taking the bus in and staying at Max's aunt's place nearby. She was memorable herself, short and husky, with brown skin and a weathered face that spoke of long days spent picking in the fields. Her pixie haircut gave her a tough, no-nonsense look, but her voice was all comedy, like she was born to star in her own sitcom.

She was also the first openly proud lesbian I'd ever met. She carried it with ease, no explanation, no apologies.

The bus trip took several days, and the wait was exhausting. Every hour dragged by. I sat with the ache of anticipation, just hoping that Rick would really come back.

He did, but his visit would be different. Rick belonged to a quiet little town where everyone knew your name. I lived in a forgotten pocket of the city outskirts where people kept their heads down and their hearts guarded. We came from different worlds, but somehow, he still felt like my best friend.

He entertained me with ideas of me moving to McAllen. He told me his sister would love having a friend like me, and his mother was the sweetest mom in the world. He romanticized Texas, and I fell hard. I was ready to go. I knew where my dad kept his wad of secret money, and I was ready to visit the Greyhound station and buy my one-way ticket out.

The two weeks unraveled faster than I could imagine. Before I knew it, the visit was almost over. In those last three days, Rick hugged me in a way he never had before, like he knew something I didn't, like maybe this was goodbye for real. I held on, my hands in the pockets of his hooded sweater, not ready to let him go. I could've cried. Maybe I did. There were so many things I wanted to say, but the words stuck like gum to my shoe. *Don't leave. Take me with you.*

I wanted to tell him how he made me feel visible, how our late-night talks were the only thing keeping me from going numb. I wanted to tell him how much I hated my life, what a jerk my dad was, how I had to visit my neighbor's house just to take a damn shower when the water was out, and how lonely I was. I wanted to tell him to take me with him.

But I stayed quiet.

It would've fallen on deaf ears anyway. He took a single step back, and with it, gently broke my heart. His hands cradled my face like something fragile, and he said softly, *"I'm eighteen. You're not."* It was the beginning of goodbye.

"I can't be anything more to you. It's not right. I'm sorry," He continued.

They were some of the coldest words anyone had ever said to me. I cried in secret, just like I always did when I felt sad.

He tried to hug me, to offer something like comfort, but my anger surged up, louder than my ache for closeness. I shoved his arms away and ran, blinded by tears I refused to wipe. I sprinted up the dirt road, stumbling over potholes and shame, and climbed through the bedroom window I used to sneak out of, now using it to escape the world instead of chasing it.

I couldn't let anyone see me like that, wrecked. Rick was a gentleman. And I was just a girl who didn't yet understand the weight of age or the sharp lines of what's allowed and what isn't. Rick left, and my innocent heart sat lonely in my hands.

Then, weeks later, a letter arrived. It was from Rick.

I stared at it for three whole days, afraid to open it, afraid it would hold another soft goodbye, this time in ink instead of words. But it didn't. Inside was Rick's voice, gentle and familiar, carrying another promise that he'd stay in touch, and that when I reached the magic age, I could take the bus to him, and we'd finally be free together. It was everything I wanted to hear.

But it wasn't meant to be.

It was nothing more than a slow goodbye dressed as false hope.

I wrote him back with a heart that felt heavier than I'd ever known. I was searching for clarity. I asked him if he was willing to wait, truly wait. And if he wasn't... then please, don't write ever again.

I never made it to McAllen.

The Queen's Pillow

I didn't have many options for safe places to run to when the world felt too heavy or when I just needed to disappear for a while. Most of the time, it felt like I was always running from chaos, from silence, from people who didn't know how to love me the way I needed. I was always searching for somewhere I could breathe, somewhere I could just *be*.

That changed the day my grandmother—my mom's mom—married her third or maybe fourth husband, and they moved into this quaint little apartment nestled in a quiet corner of the city's noisy downtown.

The building was old, charming in the way timeworn things often are, with its creaky wooden staircases and Victorian-style doors that seemed to whisper stories as you walked past.

I never called ahead or warned her I was coming. I'd just show up. And every single time, if she heard my knock, she opened the door like she'd been waiting just for me, arms outstretched, a soft, knowing smile on her face, and a hug that said, *You're safe now.* That apartment became my refuge. Her arms became home.

Grandma Jenny was my favorite person in the world. Her life had been hard from abusive husbands, broken dreams, and years of scraping by, but none of that mattered to me. To me, she was home. She was the closest thing I had to a mother, and she loved me in all the ways that counted.

Even when money was tight, she always made sure I had something warm to eat. She'd piece together a plate from whatever she had left in the fridge and serve it like a feast. Then she'd walk over to the kitchen window above her sink, crank it open just enough to let out the smoke from her cigarette, and lean into the breeze like she was letting go of something only the wind could carry. I always wondered where her thoughts took her as she stared out at the city.

I remember watching her from the kitchen table, thinking how beautiful she looked standing there, tired but happy, worn but glowing. I couldn't believe how deeply she cared for me when she didn't have to.

She was my constant, my queen. Her thick accent, those golden eyes with hints of blue-grey, her short dark curls always set the same way since the '40s, she was something. She drank too much, smoked like a chimney, and partied without apology. But her heart was pure gold. And it loved me fiercely.

The inside of her little apartment was literally the inside of her heart. There was warmth, there were cats, there was kindness, and the most welcoming feeling I had ever felt. Grandma Jenny always insisted I sleep in her bed when I stayed over, while she and her man slept on the pull-out sofa bed in the cozy living room, watching old shows. I felt weird about this arrangement, but she insisted. It was the safest pillow I had ever slept on.

It became a kind of tradition; whenever my father's drunkenness became too much to bear, I'd run. But not to the streets anymore. I was done with that. I'd already learned what I needed to from cold sidewalks and stranger danger. Now, I ran to her. I'd catch the bus without thinking, anxious, but with something like hope, knowing she'd open the door every time I knocked. She didn't raise me, not really. But in those fragile teenage years, she gave me something I'd never had before, a place to land softly, a kind of love that felt natural and warm and real.

On Fridays, when her husband got paid, we'd walk to the market like it was the highlight of our week. We'd gather armfuls of ingredients like bright fruits, fresh fish, crusty bread, and talk about what we'd cook like it was a celebration.

Back home, the kitchen would come alive. She showed me how to choose the perfect avocado, how to chop onions with a rhythm, how to season food by instinct, not by measure. Music, always flamenco or some old Spanish ballad, blared from the speakers of her boombox. She and her husband would dance like no one was watching, twirling around each other while something rich and fragrant simmered on the stove.

She'd laugh until she cried, her voice lifting into song like it had wings. And I would sit there, just watching, soaking it all in, the smells, the music, the way her joy filled every corner of that little apartment. It was mesmerizing.

I still ache for those moments, the way it felt to belong, to be fed and seen and loved without condition. I didn't need the world to be perfect. I just needed *her*.

It was the one place I could count on—no questions, no judgment, just open arms. She protected me with everything she had, as if loving me could undo the hurt in both our lives. I used to wish, quietly and often, that my own mother had it in her to love me the same way.

When she left this world, it felt like something steady and sacred had been torn away. She left behind a silence, and a dozen hearts quietly broke to pieces.

I Don't Know Her

It was another bad day on San Antonio Street, the kind that settled into my bones before it even began. I was terrified. It was the fear that made your body go still before anything even happened. My dad, worn thin from screaming matches with my mother and nights spent begging her to come back, turned all that rage onto me. It had been years since I realized he hated me; I could see it in his eyes. The way he looked right through me like I was the mistake he could never erase. But I didn't know what to do. I *lived* there. My brothers were there. All my things, small pieces of my identity, were there. And I couldn't bring myself to leave them behind permanently.

Something small set him off, maybe a word, maybe just the look on my face, and suddenly it exploded. My tone was wrong, my expression was wrong, and I became the target. He called me a bitch. A loser. He punched through my door again, kicked holes in the walls like they had insulted him, too. He grabbed something—anything—and hit me again and again while I screamed for him to leave, for him to *stop*, for someone, *anyone*, to step in.

But no one did.

My older brother never really protected me. He stood by, silent and obedient, being the way he was trained to since childhood, trying to keep the peace, watching just to make sure no one needed an ambulance. He blamed me sometimes, told me to shut up, stop arguing back, and said it would stop if I just kept quiet. He was probably right. My attitude was trash, and I brought a lot of trouble and pain upon myself. But still, I wanted to scream at him, too, and ask how he could just watch. But I never did. Because I knew deep down, he was just as scared as I was. He was still the boy watching me get hit when we were just babies, too afraid to speak up. Nonetheless, everyone was convinced I was the problem, but I was the only one angry enough to counter the fear.

And maybe that was the worst part. That fear ruled all of us. That love couldn't grow in that house. That we were all just trying to survive in that house, in silence. And regardless of his reasons, I love him and forgive him, and I am sorry he ever had to see that bullshit.

When the beating stopped, I called my Aunt Elly, one of my mom's younger sisters, and cried as I begged her to come get me. She arrived quickly, and I climbed into her car with nothing but a backpack and a change of clothes. As we drove down the dusty road, she asked if I'd eaten. It was autumn, and night had already fallen like a heavy blanket. I was starving.

We stopped at a small shopping strip to grab some food, and that's when I saw her, my mama. She was walking toward a car belonging to a man from the neighborhood, a loser she'd started seeing after meeting him through neighbors. Without thinking, I ran up to her and shouted, "Hey!"

She froze, eyes wide with shock. For a moment, I thought she'd run to me, tell me she missed me, but instead, she turned and walked quickly to the car. I followed, tears falling as I pleaded, "Why don't you want to talk to me?"

She looked disturbed and tried to walk away in the opposite direction, but I kept following, my heart breaking with every step. I grabbed her arm and demanded, *"Where have you been? Why won't you come home?"* I needed answers. I missed her so much, but she didn't seem to care.

Then, without warning, she raised her hand and slapped me across the head. Just then, a sheriff's car rolled by, made a sudden U-turn, and pulled up beside us. Aunt Elly wrapped her arm around me, her eyes full of sorrow. "Let her go." But I couldn't let it go.

The sheriff asked if there was a fight. I shook my head. "No. She's my mom." Hoping his presence would make her soften, I looked to her. But she didn't. The sheriff turned to her, calm but firm. "Is that your daughter, ma'am?"

She looked away, cold as ice. "No. I don't even know her."

He ordered us all to leave the parking lot before pulling away. But her words hit me much harder than her hand. I collapsed to the ground, breath stolen from my lungs. Aunt Elly lifted me up and whispered, "It's going to be okay. She's just sick."

But it wasn't okay. First, my father, then my mother, the people I should have been able to count on, had broken me in a single night. I felt empty, erased. Like I was born into trash and couldn't even find a place to be thrown away.

Tiny Dancer

My mom had six sisters, and most were scattered across the country and the world, like confetti. I didn't blame them. The options were either backbreaking field work or city life that chews you up, spits you out, and then sends you a bill for emotional damages from years of fuckery.

But Aunt Reyah? She was a whole different species. A dreamer. An adventurer. A "married-for-five-minutes" kind of gal who learned quickly that just because something sparkles doesn't mean it's not wildly toxic.

After her whirlwind divorce at the ripe old age of 22, she packed her bags and moved to Paris. Yes, *that* Paris. I never had a clue what she actually did there, but as a child, I could only imagine she maybe ran away with a mime. Every so often, she'd send gifts and postcards through Grandma Jenny, like an international fairy godmother.

One day, when I was about six, she sent me a book. Not just any book—*a ballet book*. In French. At that point, I couldn't read particularly well in English, let alone a language that looked like cursive. But that didn't stop me. I flipped through every page, mimicking the poses like I was born in the Bolshoi.

I was already known in the family for walking on my tiptoes as a toddler. Grandma and the aunts used to call me "the little ballerina" or "tiny dancer," which I took very seriously. We were sharing a house with another family at the time, and the only hard surface I had to practice on was a narrow strip of tile in front of the fireplace. But to me, that little hearth was my grand stage. I'd twirl until I was dizzy, performing for an audience of none, and loving every second of it.

Word got back to Aunt Reyah, and in true fairy god-aunt fashion, she sent money for ballet classes. It wasn't much, but it was enough to get my little slipper in the door.

On the first day of class, my dad dropped me off in a rugged pair of hand-me-down shorts, a tank top, and the ugliest pair of waffle-stomper boots. I was practically dressed for a camping trip, not a plié. But I was too excited to care. The instructor gave me a once-over and smiled sweetly, like, *"Bless this child."* She rummaged through a closet of leftover costumes and found a leotard and slippers that *mostly* fit. I changed, joined the class, and floated.

I only went for a few weeks. Aunt Reyah eventually disappeared into her next great mystery—maybe Italy, maybe Morocco. But those classes stuck with me. Even after they ended, I practiced everything I'd learned again and again. No YouTube, no TikTok tutorials, no fancy studios, just a little girl spinning on tile, dreaming big inside a house full of troubles.

In a world that often made me feel invisible, dancing gave me something I could claim as mine. I didn't need a stage. Just a spark. And Aunt Reyah gave me that. I never stopped dancing, and I never will.

The One Hundred Acre Wood

The building was a tall, tan adobe-style structure, topped with faded Spanish roof shingles and divided into eight small apartments. We lived in Apartment One, downstairs, right next to a narrow patch of grass that sat tucked beneath the staircase leading up to the second floor.

Directly across from us lived Arielle, a girl my age whose parents were strict Jehovah's Witnesses—quiet, watchful, always keeping her close. Kitty-corner from our unit was Michelle's place, a young kindergartner just like us, but already an athlete in softball and soccer.

The building itself was shaped like a square, missing one side at the open front, acting as an entrance. At its center sat a large, round patch of grass, our play yard, ringed by a cement walkway that looped to each apartment's doorstep. It was the kind of place where everyone saw everyone, whether you wanted to or not.

Helen was a teenager from Portugal who lived across the street on a small farm. We shared the same dead-end road, and sometimes we'd wave or say hello, but my favorite neighbor lived upstairs—right across from us. His name was John.

That apartment meant everything to me. It was the first real home we ever had with my mother. Not a borrowed couch. Not a friend's spare room. Not another grim motel. It was ours. We had our own kitchen, our own fridge, a TV, and a front door we didn't have to knock on to enter. For the first time in my young life, I felt like a person. I believed we would live there forever, that nothing could take it away.

John was unlike anyone I'd ever known. He was an artist, always working on stone busts that looked like actual people, with opera music echoing out of his apartment like a soundtrack to something bigger than this dusty little complex. He made casual small talk with my older brother and me, and he was always kind and respectful to my mother, something we weren't used to seeing.

Tall, blonde, mid-fifties maybe, with wire-frame glasses and a quiet air of mystery, John didn't fit into the world around him. He didn't look like the tired farmers or the drunks my parents kept company with. He had a surfboard leaning up against his porch wall, and a car with racks strapped to the top, like he was always one step away from an adventure.

To me, John wasn't just a neighbor. He was fascinating. Different. A reminder that something bigger and better might be out there. In my eyes, he was the most interesting man in the world.

I used to spend the day visiting Helen, collecting eggs from her hens, checking on her garden, and keeping one eye on the street, waiting for John's blue sedan to pull up so I could rush over and ask him all about his day like a nosy little reporter.

Helen spoke broken English and was fluent in Portuguese, but somehow, we always understood each other just fine, usually with a mix of words, pointing, and a lot of laughing.

I'll never forget this one cringy day. I had just finished gathering eggs and was running across the street to drop them off before catching John as he unpacked his car. But as I ran, I noticed something odd, something felt shaky in one of the eggs. I stopped mid-step, my eyes got big, completely convinced there was a baby chick inside.

I turned and hollered, "Helen! What's in it?!" Raising the egg up to show her.

She looked at me curiously and yelled back with a silly little giggle, holding her hands to her mouth like a megaphone, "Yolk!"

I froze, confused like a deer. *Yolk?* What even was that?

Still clutching the egg like it might hatch at any second, I ran to my mom, totally panicked. "There's yolk inside!" I squealed, thinking I was delivering urgent scientific news.

She laughed. I didn't get it.

Enough rambling.

Once John got to know us better, he started inviting my brother and me up to his apartment. I remember how his kitchen table always looked. It was cluttered with papers, pens, and bits of who knows what. It didn't look like anyone actually ate there. It looked like a workspace for a mind that never turned off.

His living room didn't look like a living room at all. A large desk sat in front of the window, and on top of it was something I'd never seen before, a big, bulky computer, glowing softly. Nearby was another table, long and rectangular, covered with clay dust and half-finished sculptures, each one with a face, frozen mid-thought.

John was a serious man. Quiet. Private. I never fully understood why he took a liking to us. Maybe he was lonely, too. Maybe he was also trying to escape a world that had let him down.

The only glimpse I ever got into his personal life was a photo of a young man tucked carelessly among the mess on his desk. "That's my son, Kyle," he said once, without looking up. "I haven't spoken to him in a long time."

John didn't like questions. If we asked too many, he'd shut us down, sometimes with a cold tone, sometimes just flat-out rude. We learned not to push. But still, sometimes, he hurt my feelings without meaning to.

I remember once seeing a nearly finished sculpture on his desk. It had strong, familiar features, more human than the others. I pointed to it and asked, "Is that someone real?"

"That was my father," he said.

Without thinking, I blurted out, "Did you love your father?

There was a pause—long enough for me to feel it—and then he snapped, "Of course I did. Stupid question."

I went quiet. The words stung more than he probably realized. What a shitty thing to say to a kid. What an asshole. In that moment, I learned something important about him, and about myself: some questions carry more weight than I knew how to handle. And sometimes, silence would have served better.

We didn't give up on John, and somehow, he didn't give up on us either. That summer became a strange little pocket of joy, filled with water hose ambushes, half-melted popsicles, and endless hours spent sitting on his staircase, swapping goofy stories like we were old souls trapped in kids' bodies.

And when he let us into his sacred upstairs apartment, which felt like entering another dimension, we escaped into a faint smell of wet clay and mystery. He'd be sculpting at his table, opera music blasting like it was a live performance just for us, while we hunched over his enormous computer like baby hackers on a mission.

"Check this out," he said one day, with a proud grin, sliding a floppy disk into the computer.

The screen lit up with the most pixelated thing I had ever seen, Winnie the Pooh and Tigger bouncing around the Hundred Acre Wood like blocky superheroes. John showed me how to work the keyboard, how to read the little thought bubbles, and how to make the characters move through the game.

"Just follow the Hundred Acre Wood, and you'll be alright," he said, as if giving life advice.

And I did. Every chance I got, I'd lose myself in that silly little game, wandering around with Pooh while some dramatic Italian tenor belted heartbreak through the speakers, and John chiseled quietly nearby. Somehow, it all made sense. A little chaos, a little art, a little honey-loving bear, it was special.

I Can't Wait for My 18th Birthday

Time kept moving, the world spinning faster with each year, but on our street, it felt like nothing ever really changed. We never wanted to be there in the first place. It always felt like a step backward, like we had been dropped into someone else's memory. The neighbors played oldies from the '50s and '60s on booming car radios despite the songs being old as dust in my generation, from cars that looked like they'd been parked there since the songs first came out. They dressed like they belonged to a different decade, spoke in a rhythm that mixed English with Spanish slang I didn't understand, phrases that felt foreign and strangely magnetic. They were beautiful in their own way, strangely captivating, but to me, it all felt like rot beneath the charm, like living in a photograph that had yellowed with age.

I clung to the rare days when friends from our old neighborhoods would come by, familiar faces from what felt like a different lifetime. I longed for those reunions, for the warmth of people we used to know, whose voices echoed the comfort of a home we left behind.

Then my oldest brother turned eighteen.

I remember my dad bringing up my brother's eighteenth birthday over and over again. He wasn't being sentimental, but he was being suspicious. And that made me nervous. My dad and my brother had never been especially close, not in a way you could see. They moved around each other more than with each other. So why all this talk about a birthday?

Still, I could feel it, something was shifting in the house, in the air between the walls. It was subtle at first. A kind of quiet that felt too quiet. A distance, like a hallway, stretched longer than before. I remember my dad mentioning things, like something important was soon to happen, but it didn't really click. I usually had no say and just went with the flow, no matter what was going on.

My brother and I were practically twins, born just a year apart. Irish twins, they used to say, laughing like it was cute. We'd always been a package deal, though he, being the older one, got more of everything, like the better birthdays, the louder cheers, the special attention. I got used to that. But this birthday felt different. Like it wasn't just about him turning eighteen.

And it wasn't. Weeks earlier, my dad stayed in his room longer than usual. And though he worked the graveyard shift, I'd still see him in the house at odd hours, moving quickly, shutting doors, lowering his voice. He was hiding something, and it didn't take long for me to figure out what.

He was seeing my mom again. Secretly. *She* was planning this party for her favorite kid.

They were dating, like teenagers sneaking around in their own home, as if I wouldn't notice. As if I wouldn't feel it.

It should've made me happy, I guess. But instead, it just made me feel small. Like I was watching something I used to be part of turn into something I was alienated from.

After all that time. After all those years she was gone, she returned like a secret. A shadow behind a closed door. And somehow, he helped her stay invisible. He snuck her into the house like she was something fragile, or maybe shameful. She let him. She stayed quiet, too. No knock on my door. No attempt to see my face. No explanation.

Maybe they both knew I'd be upset. Maybe she thought it was easier to act like I wasn't there than to try and fix what she broke. But I was there. I felt every second of it. I wanted her to see me. I wanted her to hold me and say she was sorry and ask me to fix it. She wouldn't have had to ask more than once because I missed her so much. Yet she ghosted me on purpose.

Rage bloomed in my heart. Not because she was back, but because she had come back under the condition that she didn't have to see me. Her only daughter. It felt wicked.

How could they?

Then, like something unfolding behind glass, things started to shift. Aunts from my mom's side started stopping by. Cousins I hadn't seen in years popped up. I didn't know why. I wasn't told. No one said anything to me, not even a hint. Just whispers behind doors and excitement I wasn't part of.

And then the day came.
My brother's eighteenth birthday.

It wasn't just a party; it was a spectacle. It was the kind of thing people dream about, and I hadn't even known it was coming. RJ, my cousin who DJs weddings and real events, set up his turntables on our front porch, stringing cables through the windows like it was a concert. My aunts showed up with bags and trays of food, loading our kitchen with smells I hadn't smelled since childhood. The living room was buried in gifts. Cars filled every space of grass, every inch of the driveway, spilling onto the gravel road that always felt too empty before.
And nearly everyone came.

All ten of my mom's siblings. All their kids. Even her father. Even some of my dad's family. They all hugged my brother. Took photos. Laughed. I stood at the edge of it all, feeling like a stranger in my own house.

People I hadn't seen in years. People who used to know me all came back to celebrate my brother. I managed to feel extremely proud of him that day.

And she?

She acted as if she had never been gone.

She stayed in the middle of the celebration, smiling, surrounded by everyone she had left behind. Except me.

I tried to pretend I was okay. I smiled when people looked. I ate what I could. I sat beside cousins who didn't ask where I'd been or bombard me with questions about my mom. But inside, I felt like I had disappeared. Like they'd brought her back and erased me in the process.

Still... I watched the lights, the laughter, the music. I watched what it looked like to be chosen, to be celebrated. I was happy for my brother. He deserved it. It gave me some hope that people around us still cared. It was a rare happy time in decades of poverty, and I wanted to freeze it.

And all I could think was—
I can't wait to turn eighteen!

But as soon as the party came and went, so did my mother. And by the time I turned eighteen, no one even noticed, and my mother was long gone again.

Johnny

I adored Johnny when I was little. It always felt like a special surprise when he rolled into our apartment complex with his clanging metal shopping cart, overflowing with toys and action figures with missing limbs, well-loved dolls, colorful bits and pieces that still felt full of magic. After my older brother and I walked home from kindergarten, we'd scan the sidewalks and parking lot, hoping to catch a glimpse of Johnny. Some days we did. Some days we didn't. But whenever he was there, it felt like something bright had arrived.

Even when we were inside or playing in the big field behind the buildings, Johnny would let us know he was near. He'd blast his boombox, and we'd come running. That music meant joy was waiting just around the corner.

Johnny didn't speak, and he didn't use sign language either. He had his own way of communicating, gentle motions with his hands and fingers, the clink of coins to show us how much each toy cost. Looking back, Johnny was probably autistic, though we didn't know that word then. We didn't need to. To us, he was simply Johnny, a kind and familiar guy, with his scruffy beard, soft eyes, and that big, beautiful smile that could light up a whole courtyard.

My mama loved Johnny. Her heart was so big, it made room for people others often overlooked. She always told us not to stare or laugh when Johnny made sounds we didn't understand, or when his hands moved in ways we hadn't seen before. "Be kind," she said. "Johnny is special." And because mama said it, we believed it.

When Johnny came around, we were thrilled. Mama would dig through drawers or check the bottom of her purse to find spare change so we could buy something small, supporting Johnny while filling our room with strange and wonderful treasures. A few neighbors didn't pay him much mind, but Mama always did. Every single time.

Johnny was my first experience meeting someone who was different in a way I couldn't explain, but it never felt strange or wrong. It just felt like he belonged with us. We didn't ask why he didn't speak. Mama didn't treat it like something to be explained. She treated him with love and respect, and that was all we needed to understand.

I carried that feeling with me. By the time I got to fourth grade, a teacher asked if I'd like to volunteer in the special education class. Without hesitation, I said yes. The kids reminded me of Johnny. They had that same light, that same magic. And I remembered how much joy Johnny brought to our little world, and how good it felt to be kind, just like Mama taught us.

I didn't know it at the time, but God was preparing me for something big.

The Smell of Bread

When I was five, Trade Market felt like the best place in the world. I couldn't imagine anything better. It sat just two blocks from our apartment, and Mama would walk us there along the streets of Little Portugal. The smell of fresh bread drifted from the bakeries on every corner, filling the air with warmth and comfort.

We'd stroll past shopfronts and familiar faces until we reached the market, where we picked up snacks, fresh meat from the butcher, and sometimes Mama's smokes. It was a routine I looked forward to, simple but full of life.

After a few months, Mama seemed to know everyone in the neighborhood. People stopped to talk, smiled when they saw her coming. My dad was away in Oregon for work, and we never heard a word from him. No letters, no phone calls, no visits. The neighbors understood. They knew she was doing her best, raising us on her own. She worked when she could, taking small jobs at laundromats or theme parks, but mostly we lived on the check Dad sent each month. It wasn't much, but it was something.

When my older brother turned six, Paul from the shoe repair shop gave him a small job at his dad's store, Lalo's Shoe Repair. Mama would drop him off for a couple of hours, and he earned a dollar a day. It meant the world to us.

But my brother's job at the shoe repair shop wasn't to earn money. It was just for fun and to give him something to do. He could be a difficult kid. He desperately needed the mentorship of a man. School was tough for him, and he was an eloper. He'd take off from Mama's hand when he felt frustrated. We all felt frustrated. But Mama didn't bring him to the doctors. We probably didn't have health insurance, or even if we did, I doubt we had money for co-pays.

When she got overwhelmed, she'd go to the big Catholic Portuguese church down the street and talk to a priest. It was tall, like a mountain. It was full of crosses and windows, and beautiful architecture that made me feel like we were walking in a castle. That was her version of counseling. I saw her cry there many times.

Mama didn't have much guidance growing up, and she didn't know how to break a generational curse. She was abused by her father, and we knew very little about him; we only saw him a few times. Grandma left him before we were born. I never judged, I just tried to understand and make sense of the relationships around me.

But the weight of those things usually faded for me once we were back outside. The sidewalk would be warm and charming as ever, and the air smelled like bread again. That smell made everything feel okay. I used to think I could live off bread alone. The taste, the smell, the feel of it, even the sound it made when it was slid into a paper bag. It met all my sensory needs, like a kind of quiet miracle. I didn't have the words for that at five, but I knew how it made me feel.

I loved my Portuguese friends and their families. There was something soft about the way they lived, the way they welcomed us, the way the whole neighborhood felt wrapped in that smell of warm bread. I loved their culture without even knowing what culture meant. The bread sealed the deal. Bread didn't just feed my tummy; it fed my soul.

It Didn't Add Up

I was a lot of things as a kid, but being bad at math wasn't one of them. Math intrigued me. It felt like a puzzle waiting to be solved, something with clear rules in a world that often didn't make sense.

I looked forward to Mr. B's class in sixth grade. He was a short, animated man with prematurely balding curly hair and arms so hairy he could be a werewolf. He always wore long sleeves with a collar, but rolled them up to his elbows, like he was ready to get to work. He rarely sat down—he was constantly moving, constantly tossing out questions that kept our minds spinning. I loved his class, even if I'm pretty sure I drove him a little crazy.

Around that time, my attitude spiraled. I slipped into this attitude of open defiance. I was loud, disruptive, and attention-seeking. It wasn't who I used to be. But I had started hanging out with a girl who was funny and bold, the kind of person who could turn being the class clown into a superpower. I watched her and thought, *This is how I hide that I don't know what I'm doing.*

What I didn't know then was that I had ADHD. I wasn't choosing to zone out during instructions; It just kept happening. And when the time came to follow along, I didn't know what to do. I felt lost. And worse, I felt stupid. So instead of asking for help, I performed. I deflected. I acted out. Because being the funny, defiant kid felt safer than being the one who didn't understand.

Mr. B had a long Spanish last name—so long that most of us couldn't pronounce it, and he knew it. To spare himself the daily butchering, he asked us to just call him Mr. B. Of course, being the immature sixth graders we were, that quickly turned into "Mr. Butthole" behind his back. I was one of the ringleaders. He never really let it get to him, but when I pushed things too far—as I often did—he'd quietly ask me to move my seat to the edge of the classroom.

I never did the homework he assigned. It wasn't because I didn't care. I just rarely even knew what it was. I was so easily distracted during class that I often missed the assignments. I didn't know what chapter we were on or what page was due.

I wanted to be more involved, but I couldn't focus. My mind wandered constantly, and I didn't know why. I thought maybe something was broken in me, like everyone else had learned how to learn, and somehow, I missed it. And now, it felt impossible to catch up.

But I loved math.

One day, Mr. B had a long list of careers pinned up on the classroom wall. He handed each of us a small piece of paper with our names on it and a bit of tape, then told us to place our name next to the career we wanted to pursue when we grew up.

The room buzzed with excitement. Most of the kids chose to be teachers. A few picked a doctor. Others wanted to be veterinarians. I stood there feeling embarrassed. I hadn't even thought about my future like that. No one had ever told me I could be any of those things. At home, I was too busy trying to adjust to the reality of our new neighborhood, which felt more like a prison, I imagined, than a place to grow up.

Unsure of what to do, like a fool, I walked up and stuck my name next to the letter "A" in the word *career* that was cut out and decorated above the display.

Mr. B looked at me, half-amused, half-confused.

"That's it? You want to be the letter A?"

"Yeah," I replied, humiliated.

He pressed his lips together sympathetically and stared at me for a second longer as I stared back at how ridiculous my selection was.

That Friday, Mr. B assigned an in-class exam that covered at least three chapters. I always took so long on tests, expecting to bomb them anyway.

I don't remember how many math problems were on the test, but it felt endless. Still, I tried to stay focused, worked through each question carefully, and finally turned it in. When I handed it to Mr. B, he gave me a suspicious look, like he thought I had guessed my way through it.

A week passed, and I had completely forgotten about the exam until Mr. B brought it up in class.

"I finally graded everyone's exam," he said, "and I have exciting news."

He paused, then continued.

"We had a lot of A's and B's, but I want to give a prize to someone who got every single question correct. Does anyone want to guess who it was?"

Some students immediately shook their heads. A few complained, saying it wasn't possible. No one could get every question right on that test.

Other students began tossing out names like the smart, quiet ones who were always studying and aced every assignment. Mr. B just kept shaking his head.

"No," he said, again and again.

He paced around the room while we tried to solve the mystery. Then he dropped a clue that made everyone pause.

"This student never turns in their homework," he said, "but was the only one to get every single question right."

A few students turned toward me. I heard one whisper, "Oh, definitely not her."

I kept my head down, not even letting myself consider that it could be me. In truth, I was hoping it wasn't. Because if it *were* me, then people would start to see a side of me I had worked hard to hide. They'd realize I was smart, but had been acting stupid. My armor would fall away, and everything would change.

And I was terrified of that.

Mr. B held the stack of exams and slowly walked down the aisle. He stopped at my desk and laid my test face up in front of me. I didn't look at him. I couldn't. I just stared at the big, bold 100% written at the top.

I felt proud. But more than anything, I felt unworthy. There were better students who deserved this.

Once the class recovered from the shock, Mr. B handed me a candy bar as a prize, then launched into a review of the exam. I could still hear whispers behind me—students snickering, struggling to believe *I* had scored perfectly.

Before I walked out, Mr. B stopped me and asked, "If you're doing your homework, why aren't you turning it in?"

"I don't know," I said. My voice cracked slightly. A feeling of wanting to be a good student, and not knowing how, overwhelmed me for a second.

And I meant it. I didn't know. Sometimes I didn't do the homework at all. Other times, I just couldn't follow through. I got distracted so easily. I'd read the same thing over and over again, unable to focus, and then have to start over. Again and again, until the repetition made it muscle memory.

That was my process.

I didn't realize it then, but I wasn't lazy. I wasn't dumb. I loved solving problems. I loved puzzles. Math was like a mystery, and I wanted to crack it. It just took me longer than most, but once I figured it out, I got *really* good at it.

Math wasn't dumb. And neither was I.

The Snoopy Cake

My dad was always a tough guy on the surface, but his mind had cracks you could see through. And there was one thing he loved above everything else, and it wasn't me.

He adored his goddaughter, Melanie, with a devotion that felt immeasurable. She was six years older than me, the first girl to ever steal his heart. She belonged to his oldest sister, his favorite, without question. My aunt Meredith had been his caretaker, his protector, his advocate against harsh, sometimes cruel parents. He would have done anything for her, and she had shielded him as long as she could.

My aunt Meredith despised my mama, and somehow, I always ended up in the crossfire. I felt like an intruder in his life, a disruption to the time he spent with Melanie.

I remember hearing my mama complain sometimes, her voice low and frustrated, about how my dad was always visiting Melanie, even though she had a dad. He took her everywhere, bought her everything, spoiled her in ways he never did for us. Whenever he had a free moment, he would go to their house, spending the day with her and her sister, Gia. Holidays, too; he treated them like they were his own children.

I couldn't understand it. If he wanted a family so badly, why didn't he do that with us?

Melanie's house was large and carefully kept, a world of order and comfort I rarely saw. Her dad was strong, confident, clean, spoke properly, and drove a new car. Aunt Meredith worked as a secretary and always wore crisp office clothes, even at home.

I only visited a few times, but I loved exploring their house, the furniture, the decorations, and the way everything seemed in its place. I went with my dad and my older brother, but I always knew my mama hated it.

What bothered my mama the most was that Melanie and I shared the same birthday. But I didn't dwell on it. My dad wasn't around much on my birthdays anyway, so I didn't miss him—not really.

One day, he picked me up to go to Melanie's party. When we arrived, the kids ran around the yard, laughter filling the air. It was a good time, and I did my best to fit in.

Then my aunt brought out a massive white cake, Snoopy carefully piped across the top. It gleamed under the sunlight, impossible to ignore. In bold black letters: *Happy Birthday, Melanie!*

I smiled big for a second, then turned to my older cousin, the one I adored. The same one who was my roommate for the park trip. I whispered, "It's my birthday too." His eyes lit up, and he shouted to my aunt, pointing at me, "It's her birthday too!"

For a fleeting moment, I felt seen.

I saw my dad glare at my cousin, and my aunt gave a fake little giggle. She slipped into the kitchen while the adults murmured nervously. When she returned with a black marker, she wrote an ampersand—and my name—on the piece of cardboard underneath the giant Snoopy cake.

I felt a sense of satisfaction for a moment. But it wasn't my own cake, and when everyone sang *Happy Birthday*, they didn't say my name. Melanie tore open her presents. Not a single one was for me. Why would there be? It wasn't my birthday party. It was her day. And yet… somehow, seeing my name there still made me feel special, if only a little.

When my dad drove me home, I excitedly raved about the party to my mama. She sent me inside and stood outside, shouting at him for minutes. When she came back, I said, "They wrote my name on the Snoopy cake!"

"To hell with Snoopy!" she said, but I didn't mind. I didn't fully understand why it mattered then. And even now… I still love Snoopy.

Words and Sonnets

Dizzy Angels Free

It's what it is to me.

Lords and Masters too,

Rule not me but maybe you.

Air and stars above,

Hate comes after love.

Careless crazy hearts,

Stop before it starts.

Crying, feelings, lonely.

Some of those things know me.

It's what it is to me.

Dizzy Angels Free.

Those were the only lines I could remember from a poem I wrote as a rebellious teenager, during a time when I was still struggling to find myself and accept the way things were. I don't know what happened to the rest of that poem—lost in a notebook, tossed during a move, or buried under years of distraction—but those lines still echo in my mind, like a faint voice calling back from a place I once escaped to.

I started writing poetry when I was eight years old. We had just moved into another rental, one of many in a string of temporary homes that blurred together over time. As a parting gift, one of my teachers gave me a few books that were going to be thrown out. She handed them to me casually, but to me, they were treasures.

One book was filled with short stories and vignettes, simple yet powerful glimpses into other people's lives. The other book was something else entirely. It had page after page of watercolor landscapes, like hills under moonlight, bending trees, and oceans stretching into twilight. Each page was paired with a poem. The lines rhymed gently and flowed with an effortless rhythm. I was mesmerized. That book didn't just show me poetry; it showed me a doorway.

I don't remember the titles of the books anymore, but I still see the cover of one in my mind. Painted buildings, their windows lit in strange, otherworldly colors. I remember one poem in particular. The line that stayed with me was, "Like dandelions on a hill…" I read it over and over, staring at the illustration of those dandelions swaying on a hillside. They sparkled and looked like they were moving, even though they were still. It reminded me of the fields we played in as kids. My mom would pick dandelions and tell us to make a wish. After our wish, we would blow on the dandelion and Mama would say to us, "Your wish is being sent!". I wish I could remember those wishes now and try to make them come true.

Stay…

She left again. Just like she always did.

Mama came and went, over and over, disappearing without warning, then reappearing as if no time had passed. Just like he used to, back when we were toddlers—back when we still waited at the window, hoping our dad would come home.

My parents were never married, and their on-again, off-again relationship was turbulent at best. They met when they were teenagers. Different high schools, same street. Both came from families with eleven children, where chaos was common and abuse was heavy.

My mother had been hurt deeply by her father in ways no child should ever experience. She spent most of her life running, from the pain, from whatever place she thought would trap her next. When she met my dad, she saw something she mistook for safety. He had a job. He had a car. He knew how to have a good time and seemed like someone who could carry her away from everything she was trying to forget.

But he wasn't her way out. He was just another kind of storm.

They became parents too young, with no idea how to raise a child, and no one to show them how. They carried their own brokenness into parenthood, and we were left to grow up in the mix of it. We were raised in pieces, patched together by short returns and long absences, always waiting for someone to stay.

My friends dropped me off at home that evening around six or seven. The sun had already started to dip below the rooftops, and the house felt heavy with silence. A Kerosene lamp lit the room warmly. As soon as I walked in, I saw my little brother curled up on the couch, his face buried in a pillow, quietly crying.

He must have been around ten years old then.

I rushed to him, sat beside him, and did what I could to calm him down. I asked what was wrong, gently, trying not to panic.

Through shaky breaths, he told me.

"Dad locked himself in his room," he said. "He won't come out. He pushed stuff against the door."

Barricaded. That was the word he didn't use, but that's what it was.

The fear in his voice was enough to frighten me. I didn't know what had happened, but I knew that something wasn't right. Something was spiraling behind that door, and we were on the outside just watching, waiting, powerless. My dad was threatening to take his own life.

My dad always had guns, including a shotgun. He would take us near the edge of the cornfield to teach us how to use them. I didn't know what to do next, just that I had to save face and reassure my little brother that everything was going to be okay, even though I really didn't know if it would be.

My brother told me he had gone into our dad's bedroom and saw writing smeared across the mirrors and walls. It was in our mom's lipstick and of angry words, crude names. "Bitch" scrawled in red. Other things, too, things a ten-year-old should never have to read, let alone understand.

Then our dad had kicked him out and locked the door behind him.

I got up and went straight to the bedroom. I banged on the door, shouting for him to open it. On the other side, I could hear him sobbing, and the distinct sound of a bottle being tipped back, then clunking down on a table. He slurred through the door, telling me to go away, to not worry about him. His voice wavered as he gave instructions, as if he were preparing me for what to do after. After what I didn't want to imagine.

My brother was crying again, trembling on the couch. I didn't know what to do. So, I cried too.

I sat down outside the door, my back against it, hoping that just being there might stop whatever he was thinking of doing. I kept talking to him, begging him to stay, trying to hold his voice on the other side of that door.

"Just stay, Dad," I cried. "Please… just stay."

I didn't know if he was listening. But I stayed there anyway, afraid of what the silence might mean if I moved.

My dad repeatedly told me to go away, but I wouldn't. I thought that maybe there was hope he wouldn't do anything, as long as I stayed near that door. I told him I was grabbing a pillow and sleeping there all night long if I had to, but I wasn't going anywhere.

He cried. Loud, messy sobs. Again, he begged me to go. But I couldn't. I wouldn't.

Even though he had been a monster in so many ways, he was still my dad. The only one I had. And I didn't want him to disappear. Somewhere deep inside, I still had hope. I still believed he could change. I wanted him to change.

We didn't know anything about depression or those disorders. We just knew Dad was an addict. Addicted to everything that was toxic. And we knew we couldn't help him.

I kept telling myself that if we could just get through this, everything would be okay. We could move back to Texas. Dad could buy a house. We'd bring the truck and ride in the back of it, like we used to when life felt lighter. He could start his business. I'd be older by then, and I could help, get a job, pitch in. We could have a fresh start. We could be happy.

I believed it. I prayed for it. I pressed my hands so tightly to my face that my palms were wrinkled, soaked in tears. I begged God to fix it. I begged for a miracle. I didn't want to hate my dad anymore. I just wanted him to stay. What would we even do without him?

Sometime in the middle of the night, I woke up and saw my little brother asleep next to me, curled up on a pillow on the floor. The most uncomfortable floor in the world, with broken, peeling, faded floorboards that must have been installed 50 years earlier. The house was in shambles, and so were our hearts. I remember how peaceful he looked, how small, how precious. And I remember how much it hurt to know what my father had put him through.

He should have been thinking about baseball, video games, and what snacks he'd eat after school. He should have been safe in a warm bed, dreaming about cartoons and weekend plans.

But that wasn't our life. This was.

And it was cruel.

And all I could think of was how I was going to shield my brother if we were awoken by a "bang".

Food basket?

We were just toddlers back then, but somehow, we had already learned how to wake up just early enough to walk across the street and collect our "food basket."

I never really understood why they called it that. I asked Mama all the time, "Where's the basket?" She'd always smile gently and say, "This *is* the basket."
But it wasn't. It was a large cardboard box, wide and heavy. I remember how she'd stretch her arms to carry it, wobbling under the weight as she made her way back to our little shelter room.

Mama always said we had to be first in line, or there wouldn't be any baskets left. So, every morning, she set the alarm, got us up, and dressed us quietly in the dark. My big brother sometimes needed extra help, so she'd ask me to button his coat while she tied her shoes. I didn't mind. It made me feel helpful, like I was doing something important.

I can't recall every detail, but I still remember the long line of people waiting at a window that looked like a concession stand. Families walked away carrying those big cardboard boxes filled with cans, crackers, and powdered milk. Some stuffed the boxes into their car trunks, others Jack and Jill'd them down the streets to their homes, carrying one side each.

That powdered milk was the worst. I hated it. When mixed with water, it looked a little pink-tinged and didn't taste like milk at all. Even as a toddler, I couldn't understand why anyone would drink it. I refused to eat cereal because of it. I knew it was meant to fill our bellies, but I didn't care about nutrition; I just knew it was gross.

Back in our tiny room, which was barely the size of a walk-in closet, Mama would take out each item from the box and place it carefully on the shelf. She'd try to make it fun, pointing to each can and saying, "Ooh, green beans! I bet these are delicious!" She made everything sound like a treat, even when it wasn't. She tried her best to make it feel like enough.

She never wanted us in the shelter longer than we had to be. When she worked shifts at the theme park, she took us with her. We'd sit on the picnic tables while she sold cups of lemonade. Sometimes her coworkers would take my brother and me around the park, and it never felt like Mama was working. It felt like we were just out for the day, having fun like other kids.

At night, we'd make sure to get to the soup kitchen early before the food ran out. The first time I remember going was on a holiday when they served turkey. After that, when the server offered me a drum or thigh, I always asked in my shy little voice, "Turkey."

Each soup kitchen was different. Some had long tables where everyone sat and waited. Others had us walk in a line like a cafeteria. Sometimes the servers didn't see me because I was so small, and my plate wouldn't get filled. I'd watch the line move forward while I stayed empty-handed, trying not to cry. Mama would always notice. She'd get upset, then split her portion with me without hesitation. Going back through the line wasn't always an option. It had gotten too long, or the food would be gone by the time we tried again.

I remember she used to tell us, with a playful voice and a sparkle in her eye, "This food? It's made by the chefs who cook for royalty in England." Even when it looked strange or smelled odd, she'd convince us it was something special. And somehow, it worked.

Then, she'd put a dinner roll in a napkin, wrap it up, and stuff it in her pocket in case we got hungry later.

Stand Tall (song)

I know that the hardest thing that I've ever learned,

Is believing things are as they should be, even when it hurts.

And some may say this life I lived, well, I sure made a mess.

But I tell them it's just incidents that put my faith to the test.

'Cause I'm wise enough to know better, and young enough to keep on getting into silly things again and again.

And I keep falling in love, sometimes, sometimes I just wonder why we have these hearts searching for each other within.

Some folks like to talk a lot, and some others are shy like me, but that doesn't mean I can't be your everything.

And I know I'm not without flaw, and I'm not trying to be at all, but I hope when you're walkin' with me that you Stand Tall.

Stand Tall, 'cause I'm gonna need ya, to make me feel like I'm a prize winner…

Oh…everybody needs to feel like they're the reason, you're livin' …sometimes.

And I once fell in love and lost, and I didn't understand the cost, but my friends stood 'round me and clapped anyway.

And I picked up my ol' broken heart, and sewed it like a work of art, and I'll think twice next time I wanna give it away.

Give it away…

'Cause, I'm gonna need ya, to make me feel like I'm a prize winner.

Oh, everybody needs to feel like they're the reason, you're livin' sometimes.

Into the Night Again

We had just moved into a new shelter room. It was four blank walls, one creaky door, and neighbors with the same tired, hollow look in their eyes. The hallway buzzed with noise: kids running to the shared bathroom, battered women wandering aimlessly with babies hanging off their hips, all of us clinging to our invisible scraps of hope.

We didn't know where we were exactly, and we never asked. Mama always said, "This is our new apartment," like it was just a fresh start, not a pit stop between disasters. We didn't have much in that room. Just a few snacks, a change of clothes, and whatever my mom managed to carry back.

But one day felt different. We had just come back from visiting Aunt Cathy—a woman with a real home, working appliances, and a backyard that looked like a page out of a storybook. We loved visiting Aunty Cathy. Her place smelled like fabric softener and chicken soup, and her backyard had cobblestones and tangled vines that made it feel like a secret garden.

And one day she had something for us. She gave us actual *toys*. Little action figures, shiny and new, not chipped or missing arms. We were over the moon. We tucked them safely into Mama's backpack like treasure and headed back on the city bus.

The ride back was the usual loud, smelly crowd, and full of people trying to make conversation we didn't want. Mama told us not to cover our noses with our shirts because it was rude, even though the air smelled like old socks and mildew.

Strangers always told her she was beautiful, and men always flirted with my mama. Her pale skin and freckles made her stand out. One time, a guy on the bus asked if we were hers. She probably looked too young to be a mother. She nodded proudly. "They got your light eyes," he said. She smiled, but I saw the weariness behind it. I looked at her eyes, and then at my brother's. They both lit up like Amber colored gemstones with green flecks, just like mine.

When we got back to the shelter that evening, my mom wanted to drop our things off and head out to eat. I assumed we would go back to the soup kitchen, as it was our routine, but Mama had a surprise. Aunt Cathy had slipped her some cash, so instead of waiting in line for lukewarm mystery meat, we went to *Weinerschnitzel*. A real treat. We ate corn dogs and French fries at the red umbrella tables while the sun melted into the sky, feeling—if only for a moment—like a normal family. Mama let us toss fries to the pigeons, so as long as we ate too. We laughed delightfully at their cooing.

When we returned to the shelter, something felt off. As we walked down the hallway, we noticed our door wasn't right. It was cracked, hanging crookedly, and the wooden frame looked like someone had kicked it in. Mama froze. "Stay here," she said, pushing the door open slowly.

The room was wrecked. Everything we had was gone.

Our new toys? Gone.
Mama's backpack? Emptied.
Makeup, maxi pads, bus fare, food, clothes—all stolen. All we had was poverty, and now we had nothing.

Mama screamed. It was the kind of scream that came from somewhere deep, somewhere tired. She knelt on the floor, picking through what little had been left. I saw her pick up a Snickers bar and stare at it for a second. I didn't know what to do except cry because she was crying. She cried like the child she kind of was. And when Mama cried like that, we knew something was really, truly wrong.

She pulled herself together and stormed down to the front office with us in tow. She was determined to get answers, maybe even justice. But the woman behind the counter couldn't have cared less. She looked at my young mother like she was a nuisance, not a person. She tilted her head, narrowed her eyes, and said something dismissive. I don't remember the exact words, but it boiled down to:
"If you don't like it, you can leave."

So, we did.

Mama grabbed whatever scraps we had left, took our hands, and we walked out into the night with nothing but each other and the clothes we had on.

Halle Wood Avenue

We loved Halle Wood Avenue, and this might have turned out to be my dad's biggest regret.

The road was narrow and quiet, lined with little cottage-style houses that looked like they'd been drawn straight from a child's imagination. Each one had a tiny front porch with a half wall just perfect for a rocking chair, and the same triangle-shaped roof and single side window you'd find in a crayon sketch. There was a tree in nearly every yard, and laughter seemed to live in the breeze.

The house belonged to my uncle; it was one of his rentals, and when my dad came back into the picture, he rented it for us.

We loved our old home in those apartments and would have happily stayed forever, but the building was crumbling around us. It wasn't safe anymore. An accident happened there, one that left me hurt, and even now it's too painful to put into words. Not long after, the city planned to condemn the place.

Within a year of our leaving, the building was gone. Our little community was scattered, and the fields that once felt magical turned to nothing more than a heap of dust.

For the first time, we had a backyard. Not just a patch of dirt, but a real yard filled with trees, like apple, avocado, peach, and lime. It felt like our own little orchard. There was room to run, space to breathe, and more joy than we'd ever known in a home. Kids from every corner of the neighborhood came by to meet us, to ask if we wanted to play. Of course, we did. This was the dreamland we didn't know we were waiting for.

My brothers and I spent our summers down at the old abandoned railroad at the end of the block. We'd act out wild stories, play pretend for hours, and laugh until our sides hurt. There was something about that place that made us feel happy and free. It felt like we could finally live. Like the world had finally let us be kids.

Just two blocks away was a little diner where Mama would walk us to get burgers when she could. And down the street lived Miss Dolly, an elderly woman with a soft voice and a generous heart. She'd let us sing and dance on her porch in exchange for candy, and sometimes she'd invite us inside to tell us stories about her late husband, who'd gone off to war. We didn't know which war, but we listened like it was the most important story in the world. Her home smelled like old books and lavender tea, and everything inside sparkled with warmth.

Halle Wood Avenue gave us more than just a roof over our heads. It gave us belonging. It gave us space to grow and dream.

There were moments when we forgot about the trauma.

We forgot about the fights, the nights spent without a home, the constant worry, and the gnawing hunger. For the first time in what felt like forever, we felt normal, and it meant everything.

Not every day was perfect. There were still bumps in the road.
Sometimes my dad would slip up, and the peace would shatter. We'd watch from the porch or behind the curtain as the police came, wheeling him away while neighbors pretended not to notice.

But even then, the house stood steady.

Then there was the time he hit my Mama as she held my baby brother. I never knew why. She literally did nothing to provoke him. We were having a good time, surrounding the TV and laughing at an evening sitcom. And he turned and looked at her and attacked her for no reason, his hand on her face, banging it against the couch. I was startled.

I ran to my room, heart pounding, and slammed the door behind me. By chance, there was a landline in my room from the previous tenant, and I had a phone. I grabbed the receiver with shaking hands and stared at the numbers. I pressed 9.

Then I froze.

My finger hovered over the next number. I started to cry. Seconds stretched out like hours. I didn't know what to do. I just knew I was scared.

Before I could decide, the door burst open with a crash. My dad stormed in and shoved me hard across the room. I hit the floor. The phone was ripped from the wall and torn apart like it was made of paper. I stared at him doing that, just terrified. I could see his rage. I knew I had to run.

I scrambled to the window, pushed it open, and climbed out without looking back. My feet hit the ground, and I looked around frantically, and then I saw them.

My mom was already across the street at the neighbors', standing with my brothers. Safe.

For a second, I thought she had forgotten me.
That she'd run and leave me behind.
But I was too hysterical to be angry.

I felt torn when the police arrived. The neighbors had called them, and for a moment, I wasn't sure whether to feel relief or guilt. Part of me thought we needed help. The other part felt like I had betrayed my family. Our happy home, our precious little bubble, was unraveling again.

I sat there crying, spiraling, wishing it was all just a bad dream. In my head, I sounded like a drama queen. But the fear was real. The confusion was real. The heartbreak was real.

And like always, Mama took him back.

The cycle reset. Our pretend-happy life pieced itself together again, as if nothing had happened. My brothers and I swept up the mess quietly, the way kids do when they've gotten used to the aftershocks. It was a vicious cycle.

And when my dad threatened to give away our cats if Mama dared to leave him, she didn't even argue. She packed up the cats, gathered us up, and we slept in the car. We parked in playground lots, abandoned corners, or near homes of people who might feed us if we showed up later that day. And just like magic, we'd end up back home after the storm passed, as if nothing had happened, again and again.

But eventually, my dad took us away from Halle Wood for good. The walls were closing in on him. It was the unpaid fines, wrecked cars, time off work to do his community service hours, and the consequences catching up. The bills were too much. And Mama? He didn't want her to work. She said it was jealousy, but we all knew it was control.

So, we were pulled from our little slice of childhood on Halle Wood Avenue and dropped straight into survival mode.

He moved us to the ghetto. Not the glorified kind in music videos, but a real trash can kind of place. The kind where sirens wail day and night, and you can't tell if people are shooting coyotes or each other. The kind where you learn to grow up fast or fall through the cracks. It was rough, raw, and nothing like what we had known. The children and playgrounds were all gone.

And just like that, the magic of Halle Wood was gone. The laughter, the porch songs, the luxury of being a child. All gone. All that was left was field work or street gangs, and you had to pick one to survive.

Bars on the Corner, Bars on My Heart

I couldn't stand when she did this. I hated it. But at the time, it was all I had of her.

She'd come home late from their usual bar, her and my dad, if they even came home at all. It was such a regular part of our lives that we mentioned it to other people without thinking.

"Yeah, my parents are just at the bar. They'll be back in the morning."

People would blink, confused, like that wasn't a completely reasonable thing for a child to say. We didn't understand the surprise. This was just life.

To us, it was just routine.

They'd catch happy hour and stay through last call. It wasn't just once in a while; it was most nights. And it went on like that for a long time.

But Mama… she wasn't the same woman I remembered from when I was small. The one who used to make me feel safe just by being in her arms. That version of her had slipped away and faded into a distant memory, to someone I hardly recognized now.

She'd wander into my room in the early hours, after all the bars closed, half-empty bottle of whiskey in one hand, a glass in the other with ice and Coca-Cola, and sink to the floor at the edge of my bed.

She'd start crying, then talking, like I was her friend or therapist. I wasn't. I didn't want to be. I was her kid.

I didn't know how to respond. At around ten or twelve years old, I wasn't old enough for these conversations. I didn't want them. I didn't like the smell of Jack or the way her voice changed when she was drinking. And I didn't like feeling like the adult in the room.

Because in those moments, it wasn't really my mother sitting there. It was someone else entirely. An imitation of her that was blurred by alcohol and sadness.

And even though she was right there in front of me, I missed her more than ever.

She'd sit at the foot of my bed, sipping between sentences, asking questions I never knew how to answer.
"Why is my life so hard?"
"Why does he treat me that way?"
She spoke like I was her confidant, like I held some grown-up wisdom tucked beneath my pillow. I didn't. Oh well. But I stayed awake, because it was the most attention she'd ever given me.

And I had school in the morning. I was always tired. My hair unbrushed, my eyes heavy. I couldn't stay awake in class. I got snappy with teachers and couldn't explain why. Just tired. Always tired.
And still, I'd get up, with a sleepy face, splash some water on it, brush my teeth, and throw on whatever clothes were clean enough. Then, I'd march to the bus

stop with my brothers, pretending like everything was fine.

But little by little, the sympathy started to dry up. I began telling myself it was okay to pretend to sleep next time. She probably wouldn't remember anyway. And when I finally did, it felt strange. It felt assertive, and I wasn't used to that. I used to ache for her attention. Now I was turning my back on it.

It wasn't just the whiskey or the late nights. It was the way I was never the priority. Not really. She had time for bars, for him, and their drinking buddies who always seemed to come first. And then, when the nights fell apart, I became her sounding board and her daughter, only after the party ended.

I didn't want to carry her drama anymore. So when I heard the bottle knock gently against the glass, or that soda can pop open, and her footsteps coming down the hall, I closed my eyes and didn't flinch an eyelash.

And she stood there, whispered a few things, maybe for a second, maybe longer, before walking away.

I used to think I was selfish for trying to sleep, like I was ignoring her. But I was tired. I was just a tired kid who had run out of ways to make space for someone who never quite loved me back.

And it didn't feel good.

On the Res

By my mid-teens, I had learned new ways to run. I was tired of the streets, tired of chasing a family that didn't exist and pretending to belong where I never really did. When my mom's younger sister, Tana, came drifting back through town on one of her visits, I saw my chance. She was always moving, always searching for family in her own way, and without thinking twice, I asked if I could go with her.

I hardly knew her, but she didn't ask questions, and I didn't offer explanations. It felt like an unspoken agreement, a silent nod that said, *We're wanderers, this is what we do.*

Aunt Tana wasn't much older than me, but I admired her. She was the family's golden one, young, beautiful, untouched by the addictions and scandals that had stained the others. She carried herself with a confidence that felt rare, and I wanted to be near it.

When her trip was over, she came back with her family to collect me. I hadn't seen my dad in two days; jail had likely swallowed him again. I scribbled him a note and told my brothers I'd be gone for a while. In truth, I wasn't sure if I was coming back at all. I only knew I needed to leave. Maybe once I got there, wherever *there* was, I'd figure out if it was a place I could stay.

My bag was small and barely filled. Tana looked at it and asked gently, "That's all you're bringing?"

I nodded. "It's all I have."

She didn't press further. At the time, she had just remarried, and there was something soft about the life she was building. She and her children seemed genuinely happy, settled in a way I had never known. Her new husband was a Native American man who lived on a reservation.

I didn't know what that meant. I had never seen one before. But I knew it was a chance to step into something different, maybe even something whole.

We drove from dawn until evening, finally pulling into a one-stoplight town where patches of snow clung stubbornly to the ground. Snow was something I had never seen before. It startled me with its quiet, its unfamiliar weight against the world.

I felt nervous, unsure what this new weather meant for me. I had never known this kind of cold. The whole town struck me as gray: lifeless grass, a sky heavy with clouds, houses that leaned tiredly against the wind. The buildings had no color, no charm, and there wasn't a single place that looked like it might hold laughter or music or light.

And yet, I told myself I could make it work. I convinced myself I could slip into their lives as easily as I had with other aunts before. Looking back, I cringe at that assumption. The thought embarrasses me now, but at the time, it felt like survival, that I could find a place, any place, to belong.

My aunt showed me to a room, explaining that her mother-in-law usually stayed there. She told me that it was mine for as long as I wanted. I set down my small bag, standing in the quiet, unsure of what to do next. I looked out the window to a night that was gradually falling. It looked bitterly cold, and there was no view.

Later, I called my brother. His best friend Marty was there too. Marty had always been like another big brother. He was a steady presence in our crowded, chaotic life. He was a couple of years older, already driving, and already carrying himself like someone who could protect us. My brother and Marty questioned me about my choice. They kind of seemed worried. But I assured them, again and again, that I was okay, that I wanted to be there. They knew just how hard life was for a teenage girl back home, but they also knew how vulnerable it made me.

The truth was, I was just hoping this place, gray as it seemed, might finally give me something different, even if I didn't yet know what that would be.

The next morning, the sky turned white and snow fell hard, swirling in the wind that howled against the windows. I watched children bundled in thick coats and mittens play outside, laughing and shrieking as though the cold were a game. I, on the other hand, mostly stayed inside, sitting on the bed, staring at the walls. I hadn't come here for fun. I came to escape and to step away from the disaster my home had become and try, somehow, to be someone new.

That evening, Tana called me for dinner. We sat down together at the table, something I hadn't done with my father in what felt like forever. Her children giggled at me between bites, asking curious questions, and her husband studied me quietly, speaking with a cautious kindness, as though he wasn't sure whether I was just a troubled teenager or simply an unwanted one.

The following day, they tried to draw me into their world. They suggested I meet another teenager from the tribe. Her husband suggested his friend's eldest daughter. Tana shot me a look that carried something between warning and protection. I trusted her instinct and politely declined.

Over the next few days, she kept me close, showing me around, introducing me to family and neighbors. We had lunch at a tiny diner on the Res, where I tasted the most delicious potato dish I'd ever eaten, something between a dumpling and a tater tot, called a Picadilly. I still remember the warmth of it, how something so simple could feel like comfort.

Tana lived life on her own terms, and I admired her for it. She let her kids drink coffee for breakfast and didn't flinch at anyone's judgment. She wore whatever she pleased, whenever she pleased. If a man disrespected her, she walked away without a second thought. I hoped she would never change.

Then, one day, her husband came into my room. I was sitting on the bed with a book when he settled into a chair across from me.

"What's your plan?" he asked.

I froze, staring down at the page as my thoughts scattered. I had never been good at looking adults in the eye, and now the question felt too heavy to hold.

"I can take you to meet my niece," he went on. "Maybe she could get you a job at the cinema."

"Okay," I mumbled, nodding like I understood.

But inside, I was terrified. I had never had a job yet. I hadn't even realized it was something I was supposed to think about. I didn't know what season it was, or when school would start again. And here was this man, kind but firm, asking me to plan a future I couldn't even imagine.

I nodded again as he explained what he thought I should do, the expectations he had for me. His voice was steady, polite. But appeared more like an authoritative figure, and I wasn't appreciating that.

Suddenly, I felt like an intruder. Unwanted. As though I'd been invited in, only to be quietly shown the door. In that moment, the warmth I had begun to feel diminished, replaced by insecurity I couldn't shake.

I don't think he ever told Tana about that conversation.

The next evening, we were all curled up on the floor of the living room, blankets wrapped around us, a crisp fire crackling in the hearth, movies flickering across the screen. It felt almost cozy, almost like family. Then one of the kids, curious and unfiltered, asked how long I was staying.

Before I could answer, Aunt Tana hushed them quickly. "Don't be rude," she said. But the glance her husband gave me told me everything I needed to know. My time there had run out.

A few days later, I called my brother in a panic and begged Marty to come get me.

"Are you crazy?!" he said, his voice sharp with worry.

"I just don't belong here," I told him, frantic. "I need to go home."

He didn't have a way to get me, but promised he'd figure something out. I told him I'd wait two days, and if he couldn't come, I would walk to the truck stop off the Res and hitch a ride. That was the way it was. I was a child unaccounted for, untracked, and unloved.

The next day, Marty called back. He'd managed to link up with a friend, and together they rented a car. "Help's on the way," he said. Relief and guilt tangled in my chest.

I didn't know how to explain my leaving to Tana. I couldn't bring myself to tell her the truth, that it was her husband's quiet pressure that made me feel unwelcome. Instead, I let her believe I was simply homesick, scared off by the loneliness and the cold. It was easier that way.

When Marty and his friend finally arrived, the weather was too bad to head out right away. Tana insisted they stay the night, and so they did. I don't think I slept at all. I lay awake, listening to the house creak against the wind, thinking about the drive ahead and wondering if I was making a mistake.

By morning, we sat together for breakfast. I kept my eyes low, afraid that if I looked up, I'd lose my resolve. Because deep down, I wanted to stay. I wanted Tana to teach me how she had started over, how she found happiness in a life she carved out on her own terms. I wanted someone to steady me, to show me how to stand.

But I didn't know how to ask for that, and I didn't understand what it would take.

So, I left the Res half-relieved, half-heartbroken.

I don't remember much of the long drive back, only the blur of roads and the sting of the tickets we collected along the way. Marty and his buddy didn't say a word about it. I hoped they wouldn't. I felt like a burden. I asked for such a huge favor, and I had nothing to offer in return, not a dime to my name, and nothing of value to give.

"Hot" Bread

I met a boy once, and at the time, I was too naïve to realize that's all he really was, a stupid boy.
He took me out to lunch at some kind of salad buffet, though I made sure to pay for myself. I never liked feeling like I owed anyone anything.

At first, I thought maybe I liked him. But the thought of letting him in too close wasn't something I could even imagine, so I told myself maybe we'd just be friends while I figured it out.

I'm not sure we dated, and I still don't know what the attraction was. He was like a hidden evil.

The salad bar itself was beautiful, green and fresh, full of vegetables I'd never even heard of. But the bread was what caught me.
There were rows of it, rye, sourdough, white, wheat; it didn't matter. I loved every piece of bread, especially with butter. I had soup, sure, but mostly I filled up on bread, like I always had. Bread had been a kind of comfort to me, like a memory etched into me from childhood.

And for some reason, maybe instinct or habit, I tucked one soft dinner roll into a napkin and slipped it into the pouch of my hoodie. My mama used to do the same thing, and I guess it just felt right not to waste it. The restaurant had a no-takeout policy, but to me, it wasn't stealing. It was saving. It was remembering. It was carrying a little piece of comfort with me.

Then he did something that turned my silly little act into something sharp.
Without asking, he slid his arm around my waist and shoved his hand into the front pocket of my hoodie. That's when he found it.
He pulled it out and shouted, laughing, "Did you take a dinner roll?!"

I wanted to disappear. Of course, I took it. But he wouldn't stop laughing.
I rushed to the car, praying he'd let it go, but he kept pressing. He kept shaming me.

"Why take a roll when there was a grocery store right outside? Why wrap it in a napkin? You're acting like a bum!"

He didn't see the truth.
He didn't see that maybe it wasn't about the bread at all. Maybe it was about the memory of walking with my mom and brother to the corner store, about how bread was warm and satisfying when not much else was. Maybe it was about how food insecurity brands itself into you so deeply, you carry it into places where you don't even realize until it's making you act bizarre.

For years, I used to ruminate on that day, embarrassed at myself for something so small. But now I can see it wasn't silly. He was just an asshole. It was proof that even when life felt uncertain, I still found something that was certain. Bread was wonderful. And that's all I really know.

Pushing the Van

Marty was my brother's best friend in the whole wide world — and probably still is. Out of all the boys that came and went in our house, he never took without giving back. He was the only one of his siblings born on American soil, which meant his parents held him to higher standards. But Marty was different.

He was a good kid with a bad-boy edge. He was respectful around me and certain adults, but a complete menace when he was with my brothers. Two years older than my brother, the two of them were inseparable, like conjoined twins. They did everything together.

Marty lived in a double-wide surrounded by trees, just past the cornfield beside our house, and the two of them would hop fences back and forth instead of wasting time walking around the maze of fields. To me, Marty was like another big brother, and no one ever thought of him otherwise. His parents, though, carried a deep disappointment in him. He didn't shine in school, never played sports, and spent most of his time getting into shenanigans with my brothers.

One night, I asked the boys to take me to the all-night fast-food joint. Marty had a license but no car. He grinned and told me he'd do it if I helped him sneak his dad's van out of the driveway. This was nothing new. My brother and I went to the front, pushing with all our strength while Marty steered. The van was old and loud as hell, and Marty didn't want to risk waking his father, who had forbidden him from using it with friends.

Once we'd pushed the van far enough from the house, Marty fired it up, and we all piled inside. We cruised into town, the thrill of getting away buzzing in the air. My stomach was set on food, but my brother and Marty had other priorities.

As we rolled through the city streets, they spotted a couple of girls their age walking along the block.

"Duck down!" my brother hissed at me. "We want to talk to them."

I dropped out of sight while they leaned out the window, calling to the girls. What I didn't expect was for the girls to actually climb in. Suddenly, I was crouched beneath the back row of seats, holding my breath, waiting for some kind of signal.

It was strangely quiet now; too obvious they were hiding something. And I was just wondering if I was still going to get something to eat now that we had company. I heard my brother whisper, "Are we still going?" followed by muffled laughter.

Marty finally pulled in the long line at the drive-thru and asked, "Do you know what your sister wants?"

"Uh, yeah... not sure," my brother muttered.

"Okay," Marty awkwardly replied, moving forward.

The girls kept chattering, asking what the plan was, and I was starting to get annoyed with being trapped under the seats like a stowaway. Then Marty hit a speed bump in the line. Hard.

"Ouch!" I blurted before I could stop myself.

Instant silence. Then both girls whipped around, leaned over the seat, and screamed.

"They're hiding a girl back here!" one of them yelled.

They fumbled for the doors, panicking, while Marty and my brother shouted explanations that only made things worse. I sat up, trying to calm them, but before I could get a word out, the doors flew open. They bolted into the night, shrieking as if they'd just escaped kidnappers.

I collapsed into laughter. "You guys are in trouble now," I teased. "Those girls are definitely calling the cops."

But Marty and my brother just smirked, unfazed. For them, it was just another wild night. For me, it was dinner and a story I'd never forget.

We stayed in the fast-food line like nothing had happened. We ordered our food, and my brothers even waved at the girls who were still glaring from the sidewalk as we pulled away.

When we got back to the sticks, Marty parked a half block from his house so we could push the van the rest of the way. We parked it carefully back in the driveway, thinking it looked untouched. When we got to the porch, nearly out of breath with our bags of food, there he was, Marty's dad, standing with his arms crossed, waiting.

"We didn't go anywhere," Marty said in their language, trying to play it cool.

"Then why do you have the keys in your hand?" his father shot back.

My brother and I shrank into the shadows, trying not to laugh. Marty stood frozen, caught in the lie, and finally admitted the truth. Not once did he throw me under the bus.

His dad gave him an earful, took the keys, and went back inside. The screen door slammed shut, leaving the three of us on the porch in silence. Then Marty grinned, snatched the drink out of my hand, and said, half-joking, "You see all the trouble I get into for you?"

That was Marty, always willing to take the heat, always loyal. He and my brother were a team, finding trouble and finding ways out of it. And maybe that's why, to this day, he'll always feel like our favorite brother.

Fly

I don't think my dad ever truly wanted to be a dad. Not really. It felt like something that just happened to him. Like he was handed the title without asking for it, and he never quite figured out how to wear it.

But every now and then, like catching a shooting star, he surprised us.
And in those rare moments, it felt good.

Sometimes he'd take us to do something simple but extraordinary to us, like an unexpected outing, a drive with the windows down, a surprise stop for ice cream, or stopping to watch the planes go by. It didn't happen often, but when it did, we clung to it like gold.

We didn't really know much about what he did for work. Just that he was always around airports. When our friends saw him in uniform, they'd ask if he was a pilot or a mechanic, wide-eyed and curious. We never knew what to say.
He'd shrug and throw out something silly. "Today I'm a flight attendant," he'd say with a grin, "Tomorrow I'm flying the plane."

We didn't know if he had job shame or was just trying to make us laugh. Maybe both. But in those brief glimmers, when he wasn't angry or tired or far away, he'd look at us like we were his. And in those moments, we believed it.

We had front row seats to the sky, and it was *awesome*.

Dad had special access to the inner parts of the airport, places most people never got to see, and for a while, it felt like we were VIPs, like tiny celebrities on a secret tour.

There were mounted binoculars on a balcony, and he'd show us how to line them up just right, zooming in until the planes looked close enough to touch. He'd crouch beside us, pointing out each aircraft in detail like he was narrating a private airshow.
"That one's a 747," he'd say, squinting into the distance.
"That one's coming in from Japan."

We'd hold our breath as massive planes coasted down toward the runway, or roared into the sky like rockets. The sound of the air shifting beneath the wings was thrilling. It was loud, powerful, and electric.

In those moments, my dad seemed spectacular. Like someone important. Someone special. And because we were with him, *we* were special too.

We'd walk through the halls with pride, his coworkers smiling and waving at us. Flight attendants would kneel down and pin shiny plastic wings to our shirts— "You're one of us now," they'd say with a wink.

Sometimes they handed us little gifts, like soft blankets covered in airplane prints, or miniature model planes we'd pretend to fly with our fingers in the car on the way home.

It wasn't Disneyland. It was better.
It was Dad's work.

And for that little pocket of time, it felt like we were the ones flying. On cloud nine, as corny as that sounds.

I thought for sure I'd grow up to be a flight attendant.
I couldn't wait.

I imagined soaring through the sky, above all the noise and fighting, far from the chaos, just floating in that quiet place above the clouds with a bunch of strangers who didn't know anything about me or where I came from.
That sounded like good livin'.

And to be honest, we *loved* going to the airport with Dad. Those were the rare moments when he felt like someone we could look up to, fun, confident, like he actually wanted us around. And I remember thinking: *Why can't he just stay like this?*
Why can't he always be this version of himself?
Cool Dad. Proud Dad. The one who took us places and introduced us to his world.

We weren't difficult kids. We were good. We were curious. We just wanted a father. Not a perfect one. Just one who wanted us around.

Make Your Own Dough

So, it started because middle and high school were tough for me, and constantly bouncing from one school to another only made it worse. It felt like I cycled through every underperforming school in town, just hoping one of them would give me a real chance instead of writing me off because I struggled.

Things weren't easy at home either. If I didn't have decent clothes, I simply couldn't show up to school. If my shoes were falling apart—literally talking from the soles—I stayed home. Getting my dad to buy me anything new was a battle. He barely covered the essentials, let alone the bills. He couldn't wait for me to get a job.

I remember eighth grade vividly. My dad was in jail, and I was living with my aunt and cousins. I had to borrow clothes from them, usually strewn across their bedroom floor. I never knew what was clean or dirty, but I tried to find something decent to wear. One day, I picked out a Looney Tunes shirt and paired it with some jeans. I thought it looked cute.

But when I sat down at school, I noticed a few kids nearby giggling and shifting away from me. Then, out of nowhere, the class loudmouth, always ready with some cruel remark, yelled across the room, "Why do your clothes smell? Are you homeless?"

My face burned red.

I didn't even really talk to anyone in that class, so this was probably the first time someone had ever addressed me directly, and of course, it had to be like that.

I was furious. The fact that it came from this pasty, short little shit with thick bookworm glasses made it even worse. Like, really? Him? The kid who looked like he walked out of Mayberry?

I shot back, "No, I'm not homeless. And I don't smell."

Then I asked to use the bathroom and left school for the day. I didn't cry. I just walked back to my aunt's house, quietly trying to make sense of it all, searching my soul for answers about how I could rise above it.

And that wasn't the end of it. After that first incident, I became a target. A few days later, that same little shit-head decided to come for me again. "Didn't you wear that on Monday?" he sneered.

"No, I didn't," I snapped back. "I wore the shirt you said smelled on Monday."

That shut him up for a second, but the damage was done. Whispers had already started making their rounds. The girl who sat next to me, one of those effortlessly pretty, popular girls everyone admired, turned to me with a concerned expression.

"Hey... are you really homeless?" she asked softly, like she actually cared.

I could tell she wasn't trying to be mean. She just wanted the story. It was still gossip, even if it came wrapped in kindness.

"No," I replied flatly, giving her nothing more.

And I left it at that. I wasn't going to feed into their bullshit. I couldn't do much about it then, so I endured it until I could.

Fast-forward to when I got to high school, I couldn't take the hits anymore. The teasing, the judgment, the lack of stability—it all wore me down.

My dad, tired of me constantly asking for new clothes or shoes, decided to solve the problem in his own way. One day, he pulled up to a small, family-owned Italian pizzeria and pointed to the door.

"Go in there and ask for an application," he said. "I'll wait here."

I was nervous as hell. I'd already had a rough experience at my first attempt at working, and I wasn't ready to jump back into that world. It seemed like everyone wanted me to grow up fast, so they could free themselves of the responsibility of raising me. In my head, I was still a child. I wanted to be cared for. I was rattled by the world. Still, I got out of the car and approached the door. A handwritten sign in Sharpie was taped to the window: HELP WANTED.

Okay…

I walked in, heart pounding, and said, "My dad told me to come get an application."

A short, thick Italian woman came over and looked me up and down. "Are you able to serve tables?" she asked with a strong accent.

"Yes, I can," I answered, trying to sound confident.

"Come and sit down for a minute."

She asked me a few more questions, nothing too complicated. Then she pointed around the shop, first to her daughter, about my age, working a knock box to make espresso drinks. Then to her son and husband behind the counter, flipping pizza dough.

She told me who everyone was and what they did. Then: "When can you start?"

I started the next day. And surprisingly, I fit right in. The customers were mostly regulars, loyal and kind, and they took to me right away. For the first time in a long while, I felt like I belonged somewhere. I felt on top of the world.

Maria, the owner, paid me in cash, since I didn't have a bank account. But despite giving me a job, she wasn't exactly warm. I could tell she didn't like the attention I got from customers.

I didn't think I was anything special. I didn't wear makeup, didn't dress in trendy clothes. I had long, dark hair and the same pale skin and freckles as my mama. Still, I was a cutie.

People would ask Maria all the time if I was Italian.

Her response? Always sharp and dismissive: "Her? No way. She's just a Spanish girl."

I had always loved the Italian people and their language. My love for ballet had introduced me to its cultural influence early on, like how Catherine de' Medici had helped shape the art I was so devoted to. I held such admiration, even a kind of innocent reverence, for their heritage.

So, it hurt more than I expected when they treated me like I was disposable.

Maria knew exactly who the big tippers were, and she always made sure to intercept them. Even when I was the one who had taken care of their table from start to finish, she'd swoop in and collect the tips before I had the chance.

One time, a regular came in to pick up a pizza and pasta order. He made pleasant small talk with me while he waited. As I handed him his food, he slipped me a folded twenty-dollar bill and smiled.

"Remember," he said, "to get where you want in life, it's all about your attitude. Everything is about attitude."

I thanked him and thought about his words. But before I could even slip the bill into my apron, Maria snatched it from my hand as soon as he turned his back.

"These tips go to the kitchen," she said sharply, "because we made the food."

She didn't hand it to her husband or son. Instead, she passed it to her daughter, who hadn't made the food either.

I sometimes wonder why I didn't bother to stand up for myself. It wasn't like me. Although I wasn't extroverted, I was never afraid to say "Fuck this" and walk away.

I think the fear of coming home jobless to my dad was overwhelming. I thought of my younger brother, who relied on me for spending cash and lunch money. I thought about what would happen if I couldn't buy my own maxi-pads or clean clothes. I used to be a silent defiant, but here I was now, silently slaving away, feeling as though I had no rights.

I'd spend hours before dinner service carefully preparing the tables by laying out linens, polishing silverware, and making sure everything looked just right. I'd check the fridge to make sure we had dessert ready, and I'd jot down anything we were out of. When the doors finally opened and the lights flickered on, our usual handful of evening customers, maybe four, on a good night, would trickle in.

Despite the tension between us, Maria always made sure I was fed before I left for the night. And I loved the food. The pizza was baked in a wood-fired oven, and the crust had that perfect smoky char. The toppings were simple but rich: thick-cut mushrooms, pepperoni, and fresh mozzarella. It was heavenly.

But what truly changed me was the pasta. I never liked pasta growing up. At home, if we had it at all, it came in a can, SpaghettiO's. Watery, bland, forgettable. I had no idea what real pasta could be until Maria served it to me for the first time.

The sauce was homemade. It was thick, vibrant, and generous, not the kind that vanished into the noodles. She topped it with a scoop of garlic butter that melted over everything, leaving behind a rich, sweet, salty flavor I'd never tasted before. It was magic. For the first time, I understood why people loved pasta. It wasn't just food—it was comfort, creativity, and love. It was by far the best meal I had ever been served at the time, and I learned to eat something enjoyable for once, instead of eating just to survive.

But all of this would change, and end, and I never knew if it was my fault or theirs.

I knew the business was struggling. The place was often empty, and they'd hinted at financial difficulties. But what seemed to bother Maria most wasn't the slow nights. It was her son.

He was just a year older than me, and it was obvious he had a crush. I never encouraged it. In fact, I barely paid him any attention. But he kept trying to get mine. He was a tall, good-looking guy with a dreamy smile. Some nights, he'd come up behind me while I was standing at the counter, waiting for guests, and squeeze my shoulders with a smirk. "Aren't you tired out here?" he'd say.

I never knew how to respond. I was scared to engage with him. I was scared of disrespecting his parents, scared of overstepping. I was like a trained little worker bee, trying not to cause problems. But he didn't stop.

One night, he lingered near the barista station, making small talk while I worked. I nodded politely, and I said very little. Then Maria came storming out.

"What are you doing over here?" she snapped at him.

He just laughed and said, "Just talking." She launched into a flurry of angry Italian, gesturing toward the kitchen. He walked away, still grinning. But she kept going, shouting and throwing pointed glances at me in between. I couldn't understand the words, but I could feel it. She was trashing me.

Less than two weeks later, she called me in and handed me my last envelope of cash.

She didn't explain, not really. Just a short, "We don't need a second waitress anymore. We wish you the best."

I overheard her daughter complaining in a mix of Italian and English that she didn't want to take on serving tables. Maria barked back, "Shut up!"

I didn't argue. I didn't ask questions. I just turned and walked out the front door.

Before it closed behind me, I caught sight of her son watching me through the reflection in the glass. I didn't even say goodbye.

I walked home that night with my apron still tied around my waist, my head spinning, wondering what I had done wrong and where I was supposed to go from here.

A month or so later, we drove past the restaurant and noticed it had closed for good. The lights were off, the signs were down. It was gone. I felt bad. Maybe it was a better move for them at the time. Maybe it was inevitable.

Years later, I saw a familiar face in the crowd at a festival and couldn't pinpoint who it was. He had that same dreamy smile and was probably in his early thirties, but had no hair. He was bald now. It was her son. I giggled. BALD!

Mama Dear

The mani-pedi days. The lunch dates. The spontaneous shopping sprees. I watched other girls live them like rituals, like a normal part of their lives. But I never had that. Not once. Not with my mom.

My mother was young, radiant. So beautiful, so kind to others. But we just didn't have that relationship.
And I never understood why she didn't want a daughter like me.

I ached for her in ways I still don't have words for. The few hugs she gave me, those rare, flickering moments of tenderness, were bittersweet seconds full of comfort and torment. Because they reminded me of what could've been. What should've been.
They were the shadow of a bond I desperately needed but never had.

I wanted a mother.

I *longed* for one.

I wanted someone to link arms with in the mall and giggle over lip glosses and silly outfits. I wanted someone steady and soft, someone who'd take me out for a treat just because she missed my face. I wanted someone who noticed when I was unwell, who comforted me through endometriosis hell. I wanted a mom who saw me, who fought for me. Who loved me loud and without question.

As a teen, as a young woman, I wanted that more than anything.
And when I couldn't have *her*, I just wished someone would fill those shoes. Someone I could spend Mother's Day with. Someone who would beam when I walked in the room, who'd brag about me like I was the brightest thing in her world. Someone I could call in the middle of the night.

I wanted a place to run to, a warm kitchen like Grandma Jenny's, where I could just lie my head down and be held.

But it wasn't in the cards for us.
And accepting that—truly letting that truth settle in—has been one of the deepest hurts of my life.

I used to carry so much bitterness. So much quiet sorrow over why I didn't have what other girls had. The mom and daughter days, the warm hugs, the playful teasing from moms who actually *wanted* to be around their daughters. It was as if I didn't deserve it.

I avoided my friends' moms like they were dangerous. Not because they did anything wrong, but because I felt like I wouldn't be good enough for them either. I almost felt inferior.
Not having my mom felt like a flaw in me.

But no matter what she did, I missed her. I wanted her back. I wanted her to try to make things right, to prove that we still mattered. With each day that passed, though, the hope of reconciliation felt more distant, more fragile. I began to fear the day would come when I no longer wanted her at all, when her return would feel strange, like a guest showing up uninvited to a life she'd already abandoned.

For years, I rehearsed conversations with mom. Over and over in my head, I'd practice the words, the tone, the timing. I'd try to figure out how to ask her why she didn't care about me.
I wanted to ask her if she hated me.
I wanted to know if she ever truly wanted me, if she had ever loved me at all.
Even though deep down, I knew her answers wouldn't fix a thing, I still needed to ask.
I needed to hear the truth, even if it shattered me.

Even though she was in and out of my life, I couldn't figure out how our relationship deteriorated. It happened sometime as I became a young woman, an early teen.

I naively used to think she'd come back and be happy to see me, tell me how she missed me, or somehow be impressed with how much I'd grown. But it never happened. She just grew further away.

I'd replay her belittling comments like broken records in my mind, trying to make sense of them. Maybe it wasn't the drugs. Maybe it wasn't the alcohol.
Maybe…she just didn't like me.
Maybe she never did.
And I was too naïve to see it.

I remember once, when I was about eleven, my aunt gave me a makeup palette for my birthday. I was so excited. I put on a little eyeshadow, styled my hair

with my mom's hairspray, and walked out of the room
thinking, maybe she'll like this style.
I wasn't trying to be grown. I wasn't trying to be sexy.
I was just a little girl, trying to feel pretty. Trying to
make my mom happy.

But the first thing she said was,
"Why are you walking all careful?"

I felt like an ass.

I hadn't even realized I was walking gently, trying
to protect the delicate curl I'd sprayed into place.
Then came the second jab:
"Why do you think you're all that?"

And just like that, the moment collapsed.
I wasn't "all that." I wasn't anything.
I was just a kid, trying to be loved by her mother.
And she made me feel like a fool for even trying.

As I grew up, I started to see the pattern.
She hated my dad's sisters. She hated how bold they
were, how beautiful, and how promiscuous.
And somewhere along the way, she decided I was just
like them.
Even though I wasn't.
I didn't talk to them. I didn't even like most of them.
But I carried their blood, their looks, and in her eyes,
that was enough.

I could've told her all that I felt. Asked her every
question, begged for some kind of answer, some kind
of peace.
But the truth was carved into our story long before I

was old enough to read it:
I was part of them.
And she hated them.
So she could never love me.

I developed a complex so bad, I carried it everywhere with me. I was unable to make eye contact with anyone, unable to speak loudly, and unable to feel confident.

Even if I gave up every part of myself that reminded her of them—
Even if I tried my whole life to be someone else—
It would never be enough.

I would've traded it all…
Every tie to my father's family, every scrap of connection, just to have a real relationship with my mom.
Just to hear her say she was proud. Or that I was enough.

But sadly, it wasn't meant to be.
Not then.
Not ever.

In something like a dream, I still believe my mama loved me somewhere in her heart, locked away, unable to reach until she learned to love herself.

Salvation on the Bus

I was always up early with my little brother. Even on weekends, when my mom and siblings slept in, the two of us were awake—he'd just learned to walk and would waddle over in his wobbly way, clutching at furniture, babbling nonsense. His favorite thing was curling up next to me on the couch to watch cartoons, his tiny chunky body warm and cuddled against mine.

Some mornings, we'd wander outside to the patch of grass in the center of our apartment complex. It wasn't much, just a worn-down circle of green that was bordered by cracked pavement—but it was enough. We'd sit cross-legged in the dew, sharing dry cereal straight from the box, laughing and talking in our own baby language.

On Sunday mornings, the world around us would change. The Protestant families would emerge, dressed in polished shoes and fancy dresses, their Bibles tucked under their arms. I'd watch them load into cars, exchanging hugs and chatter, bound for church together, whole and happy. Mama only took us to church when she was sad. When my dad was around, he only took us on holidays. Most Sundays, we stayed home. Just us.

One day, the family who lived right across from us, Annie and Ben, kind-eyed and always smiling, asked if I'd like to join their daughter Arielle at Sunday school. I remember feeling this surge of warmth rush through me. Arielle was my friend. I loved being around her. Her mom used to braid my hair so gently that it made me sleepy. Their apartment was small and messy, but always smelled like fresh tortillas and pan dulce.

I'd watch the Sunday school bus every week—how it would pull up with a cheerful screech, the driver stepping out with open arms, laughing and hugging the parents. I could hear the singing echoing from the bus windows—children's voices carrying melodies of joy I didn't fully understand but longed for.

Annie asked me to tell my mom to speak with her about joining. I never did. I was too wrapped up in the dream. All I could think about was riding that bus, being a part of those songs, those hugs, that brightness. I wanted to be one of those kids. I wanted to belong. I wanted what I saw in that painting from the old room my brother and I were trapped in—the girl with the glowing face praying to the Lord. It looked like love. I wanted to be saved. I didn't know what it all meant, but I wanted that more than anything.

So, one morning, while Mama was still asleep, I snuck out. Quietly as I could, I slipped on my shoes and cracked the front door open. I thought my little brother was still asleep. But as I stepped into the hallway, I heard the soft thud of his hands on the floor. He was chasing me—half crawling, half stumbling, calling out.

I panicked. I kept whispering, "It's okay, go to Mama, I'll be back." I gently pushed his little hands away from the door, but he clung to me. His face crumpled, eyes wide with fear and sadness, and then came the crying—loud, aching sobs. But I was five. I didn't know better. All I knew was that I wanted something just for me. Something happy. Something bright. And so, I left him there, crying in the doorway.

The bus ride that I had dreamt about for so long should've been magical. The kids were singing, the sun was shining, and everything seemed perfect. But all I could do was pout. I sat there with my head buried in my lap, tears soaking the fabric of my skirt. His face haunted me—his tiny outstretched arms, the way he called after me. I felt like a monster.

The rest of the day blurred past me. I tried to play with the other kids. Tried to laugh when someone passed me the ball. I don't remember the Bible lesson. It felt like the longest day of my life.

Later, we had an outdoor service. Folding chairs lined up in uneven rows, sunlight filtering through the leaves. Arielle giggled with her friends. I just sat there, hollowed out. I didn't want to sing. I didn't want to pray. I wanted to go home. I wanted to be forgiven. I wanted to hug my brother and tell him I was sorry. I'd never made a decision like that before—choosing myself. I hadn't known it could hurt so much.

The bus ride back was quiet, at least in my memory. I think someone asked if I had fun. I think I nodded and fake-smiled. When we pulled up, Annie leaned down and smiled kindly. "Do you want to come back next Sunday?" she asked.

I didn't hesitate. "No, thank you," I said softly.

She smiled, but something behind her eyes shifted—something like worry, maybe disappointment. I don't remember her words. Just her expression.

I ran to our door, apartment one. Bursting through the door, I searched until I found him. My brother. I scooped him up and held him close, burying my face in his tiny shoulder. He didn't understand why, but he hugged me back.

That day, I learned something I'd never forget: sometimes, putting yourself first doesn't feel like freedom. Sometimes it feels like a punishment. And I learned it far too young.

I didn't know how my mom or dad did it. They never hesitated to choose themselves. It felt toxic. It felt wrong. But I was too young to understand how it worked.

Letters to Myself

A king can find the largest stone,

And give it to that only one.

And to her it may feel so plush,

But with it he can also crush.

A fairy takes a wish and grants,

While some young girl hopes for the chance.

A non-existent nymph with wings,

But I believe in many things.

As once a soldier who wrote me home,

And clutched me tight so I might feel owned.

That any such man would feel the same,

Am I just another dame?

Amber eyes with flecks of green,

That I am sure he's never seen.

Dappled face and pouting lips,

A woman's shapely, seasoned hips.

For him, I could not be enough,

And longing for a stranger's lust.

Who can hold such emptiness?

Restore my faith in mending this.

The lips that kiss can also lie,

The tongue that speaks may even try.

Can the eyes desire me as they?

Or is it he who wheels my heart away?

The War in My Heart

Being in love was never one of my strong suits. I had crushes, sure, and moments that could have been something more, but I never had a real relationship until I was about twenty-one. By then, I'd gotten used to a sort of freedom that some of my peers envied. I was single. I didn't have kids. I had my own car, a handful of acquaintances, a little money in my pocket—and I could dance.

Dance was my anchor. I had taught myself ballet in my bedroom mirror, practicing until my toes blistered. I took whatever classes I could find—classical ballet, contemporary, swing, ballroom, tap. If there was music and movement, I wanted to be in it. Dancing made me feel acceptable, like I belonged in the world. Like I was *someone*. My friends would show me off at parties, "Look at her, she dances!" and I'd feel the room shift when I moved. The boys noticed.

Still, I was restless. I kept wondering where I was supposed to fit. I bounced between jobs. I picked up side gigs teaching dance to anyone who wanted to learn. Meanwhile, life kept moving without me. My peers were getting married, having children, moving in with partners, and stacking furniture into shared apartments. They were growing up in ways I wasn't.

I thought about joining my dad at the airlines, becoming a flight attendant. The idea of travel, of drifting through different skies, appealed to me. But the world shifted—events outside my control closed that door. The military wasn't an option because of my medical condition, and I didn't have a Plan C. I was floating.

At least I had my younger brother. He was my reason, my responsibility. Troubled, lost, with our parents too absent and reckless to anchor him, he only had me. I tried to be steady, to be the one constant thing in his life. But one day, he moved in with his godparents. The world had become too heavy for a young teen who needed stability I couldn't always give.

When he left, I felt the absence like an empty stage. I wanted to be there for him. I wanted to be enough. But I wasn't.

And then, almost without thinking, I left too. I met someone and eloped. I don't know if it was right or wrong. Maybe it was neither, maybe it was both. Instead of running from the drama, I was running from a bitter emptiness. All I knew was that, for the first time in my life, someone accepted me in a way I had never been accepted before. I didn't question whether he loved me. I didn't want to. In that moment, we needed each other, and that was enough.

Not long after, he joined the Army. He went off to war, and I didn't understand then how quickly it would all change. I wanted to go back to Texas, and somehow this marriage, this new life, was my way home. For a little while, I felt settled. I had someone to share meals with, someone to watch shows with, someone whose presence filled the quiet.

But the war came too soon. The day he left, it was as if time folded in on itself—stuck, frozen, refusing to move forward. I stood there feeling as if everything had to pause, as if time could be held in place if I didn't move. I didn't want to let the clock tick. I knew that once it did, his presence would vanish into thin air, and I would be alone again. Panic set in.

That's when I began to unravel. Slowly at first, then all at once. I slipped into a place I can't fully explain even now. My mind turned against me. Intrusive thoughts clawed their way in, wild and frightening ideas taking root. Irrational fears shadowed me everywhere I went. I was convinced this was the breaking point. After everything I had already been through—things I still can't bring myself to say out loud—I thought this was the end of my rope.

I wanted help, but I didn't know how to ask. No one had ever taught me when to reach out or to whom. The idea of admitting I was unraveling humiliated me. I was ashamed. But the fear was greater than the shame, so I asked. And when I finally did, it was like exhaling for the first time in years.

I discovered I wasn't alone. There were others—so many others—who understood, who had been where I was. There was help. Real help. And in that moment, I needed it more than I had ever needed anything.

The war had been everywhere. It was on every channel, as if it were some grotesque reality show the whole world couldn't stop watching. I avoided it. I knew what his role as a cavalry scout meant. He wouldn't be behind a desk or anything like that—he'd be at the very front, in the crossfire, where danger had a name and a covered face. I didn't want those images in my head. I didn't want to imagine what could happen.

All I wanted was to protect our little boy from the truth. I wanted him to believe the world was soft and good, a place where people were kind and no one ever left. So, I painted him that picture in my words and my smile, even if my hope was crumbling.

That morning, I left my son with a sitter. I didn't want him to see the fear, to absorb the heaviness of goodbye. I wanted to protect him more than anything. I didn't want him to feel what I felt. But even now, I wish I had taken him, wish he could have had that one memory of his father in uniform before the war devoured his mind.

The soldiers stood in long, perfect lines, green uniforms crisp, black boots gleaming in the morning light. They looked still and solid, like an unshakable wall, but I knew each one had a heart pounding inside. The buses pulled in, their engines rumbling like distant thunder, and the captain began his farewell speech. His voice carried across the lot, promising to bring every man home. I wanted to believe him. Everyone wanted to believe him.

I glanced around at the wives, the husbands, the children clutching hands. The air was thick with tears and whispered prayers. Every single one of us was wondering the same thing: would they come back in boots… or in a box?

I tried to memorize the soldiers' faces, one by one, wanting to hold onto the images in case some never came home. Then I spotted him, standing there in formation, very steady, serious, a quiet presence amid the chaos. In a moment, the marching started, and without thinking, I took a step toward him. My legs felt unbearably heavy, like I was sinking into quicksand. I just wanted one last close look, something to carry with me, something I could share with my son if I ever had to. That's when I felt arms wrap tight around my waist.

It was Suzanne Shaw. Her voice was warm and steady in my ear. "I got you. It's okay. I'm here. It's okay."

Something in her touch felt almost motherly. I was so young then, so untested in the ways of adult life. Suzanne was the opposite. She was sharp, resilient, the kind of woman who'd already weathered a few deployments. She'd seen what I was just beginning to face. She held me as I buckled, my tears flowing steadily.

"Don't," she whispered firmly. "Your son needs you."

Her words cut through the fog, and something changed. I remembered: I wasn't alone. I still had our boy. And, just like with my younger brother years before, I had someone who needed me to be strong, even if I felt like falling apart. I clung to her until the shouting began, one last chorus from the platoon, fierce and defiant.

"Scouts out!"

The words echoed in the air long after they climbed onto the buses, carrying them away from everything they knew.

And the War Didn't Stop on the Battlefield

And what should have been a joyful reunion after more than a year apart was anything but.

When the celebrations faded and it was time to go home, I saw something in his eyes that wasn't relief or happiness. There was a weariness there—something cold and distant that terrified me. The briefings had warned us it might be this way at first, but no one told us it might last forever.

Many of our friends never came back. Calls would arrive, official and grim, letting us know something had happened. Communications would cut out until the dreaded notification to next of kin. We all waited anxiously, hoping no one would knock on our door.

But what was worse than him not coming home was how he came back.

I don't think he ever really came back.

He was different—lost, distant, haunted. And he scared me.

I was young and clueless, just trying to survive. I didn't understand what was wrong, didn't know how to help. Talking about it was taboo, so we both bottled it up, locked it away like a secret too painful to face.

We fought—often and fiercely. That was all we knew. That was the language of military life, the soundtrack of the war we couldn't escape. It was everywhere—in the news, in his silence, in the weight between us.

I couldn't fix it. I couldn't find peace. He would lash out, and I would fight back. The cycle was vicious and relentless.

While other young people my age were planning their futures, I was trapped trying to save myself.

I stopped dancing. I didn't go to college. I worked a part-time job just to keep things moving. I had nothing to show my son.

He would look at me with those big, searching eyes and ask, "What's wrong with my dad?" And I had no answers.

The soldier I once knew paced through sleepless nights, smoking cigarettes like they could burn away the fear inside him. It broke my heart to know I couldn't reach him. He was scared, and I was too.

It felt like he had given up on the life we tried to build, and we were stuck in limbo, waiting for a man who was gone. I tried, again and again, to pull him back.

Then, Christmas day arrived, and I hadn't really planned anything. My boy and I were mostly alone anyway. His father stayed in bed most of the week, only rising to smoke.

There was no tree, no food, no laughter filling the house.

My son woke up and asked, "Is it Christmas yet?"

I smiled and said, "Yes, let's go see your gifts!"

He raced to the living room, eyes wide with excitement. But when he saw the small pile of four wrapped boxes on the floor and the single red stocking pinned to the wall with a thumbtack, he stopped.

He looked around and said softly, "It doesn't look like Christmas."

Those words hit me like a punch to the chest.

I realized then that I had been holding my breath, waiting for him to come back from that war, but he never would. I couldn't keep living in the shadow of a war he brought home with him.

As much as it hurt, I knew I had to reset.

It was one of the hardest things I had ever faced.

Here I was, a young mother trying so desperately to be better than the past, and I was failing.

And it hurt like hell. Because, as much as I hate to say it. I didn't sign up for the war. He did. And here I was in the middle of it, and I was tired of fighting.

Letters Never Sent

Hey Dad. How's it goin'? I hope this letter finds you well. I know a lot of things weren't right when we were younger. Mistakes piled on mistakes. You pissed me off, and I pissed you off. But I never stopped being loyal to you, Dad. Not once.

Like that time about the neighbor, storming up from his little one-room cabin, ready to fight you over our dogs. You met him on the dirt road. I ran out, kicking him while you swung. Or the man who wouldn't stop running his mouth about my brothers, until I stepped in front of you with my bat. We ran him off together. I didn't care.

I wasn't the best daughter. But I still wanted your approval. I still wanted to protect you. Most of the time, you were all we had.

Like you, I couldn't make things right with Mama. But I held out hope for you. I forgave you for your wrongs, and I thought you'd do the same.

And I miss your humor. The way you could make me laugh until tears streamed down my cheeks. Happy ones. The way you'd have the whole room in stitches just by opening your mouth. That was the dad I loved most.

And on your days off, the way you'd play your guitar or the piano, and sing your made-up songs. I always wondered why you weren't a famous musician.

I'd get a blanket and cozy up next to the piano, and gently fall asleep.

Then one day, you wrote me off.

No fight. No reason. Just a careless "4 o'clock? Yes, I'll be there," and then nothing. No call. No message. No sign of you walking through those doors. You stood me up like I was nothing. And never came back.

I never really understood how you could do that to me. Maybe it was something you were used to after years of abandoning us.

I traveled over a thousand miles to see you that day. I tried to make excuses for why you stood me up. Maybe it was something I said. Maybe it was something I did. Or was it always the plan? Were you just waiting for the magical day you could write me off?

Maybe you thought I reminded you too much of a past you wanted to forget. That hurt me.

And the truth is, if anyone should've been cutting losses, it was me. I should've been the one holding grudges, demanding apologies. But I never did. Not once. All I wanted was for you to forget the ways you'd hurt me, forget the mess, and just be my dad.

You were the first man to make me laugh. The first man to make me cry. The first man to hold me. The first man to break me.

All I wanted was to sit across from you. Have a beer. Hear your stories. Watch your face come alive. Laugh until I couldn't breathe.

But instead, I'm here. Talking to a ghost who's still alive. I miss you, Dad. And I hate that I still do.

Goodbyes Never Get Old

Times were changing, and I was growing up—though in truth, I was mostly just redoing the same things, only now as an adult. I still chased fireflies on summer nights, lit bonfires with friends, and kept searching for something steady to hold on to.

For a long time, I thought of the Army as my escape, a vessel that carried me out of the place that hoarded so many of my saddest memories, like a photo album I could finally throw away. But when he joined and we moved again, it became something else: just another collection of sad goodbyes. And those never got easier, and they never got old.

Then there was her. Round-faced, olive-skinned, a year or two younger than me. She was always there in an instant, always with an open door. Another fight? Another deployment? She'd just shrug and say, "I got ya."

She was vibrant and free-spirited, the kind of woman who could light up a room without even trying. Her husband was just the same. When the guys finally came back, after what felt like the longest 400 days of our lives, we practically lived at each other's houses, celebrating with dinners and laughter every week. But while everyone else seemed whole again, I was usually there with only my son. His father returned colder, unsettled, and more distant than ever.

I tried to smile through it all, for my boy's sake, but inside I felt like I didn't feel welcomed in my own home.

So, I kept myself busy—therapy, night classes, part-time work, anything that felt like forward motion. His father hated that I went to school, but I had this goal of college, and I wasn't about to let it go.

Meanwhile, my friends grew tired of my endless excuses to brush them off, even I got tired of hearing them. "He won't like it." "He's working late." "He's not feeling well." They rolled their eyes but never stopped inviting me.

Then one evening, after class, I walked out into the parking lot, juggling books and exhaustion, only to see headlights swing behind me. Lilly's SUV screeched to a stop, and Josh and Kelly pressed up against the windows like kids on a joyride. Before I could even react, Lilly rolled down the window and shouted, "This is an abduction—get in!"

Kelly swung the back door open from inside while Josh and Lilly ushered me in like a pair of bodyguards on a mission.
"I'm going to get in so much trouble," I groaned, covering my face with my hand.
"But you're going to have so much fun!" Lilly shouted back, already cranking up the music.

I burst out laughing, caught off guard, as I slid inside. No questions asked. For once, I was part of a group. I felt like a main character. I was their friend, their girl, their family. And in that silly, ridiculous moment, I felt free.

The three of them broke into song, belting out lyrics and wiggling around in their seats like the car itself was a stage. I tried to hold onto my worry, to think about the storm that would hit when I got home—but it slipped right out of my hands. For the first time in what felt like forever, I let go. The damage was done; I was with my friends, and that was enough.

We pulled up to a crowded billiards bar, the kind of place I didn't usually go to. Lilly, fearless as always, snagged us a table while Josh and Kelly returned with clinking bottles of beer. I confessed I'd only ever played pool on my dad's old table and didn't know the rules.
"The best part about this game," Lilly hollered with her wide grin, "is that there are no rules!"

And just like that, we were laughing, drinking, and playing terribly at pool, but none of it mattered. For a few shining hours, I wasn't the worried wife or the weary mother. I was just me—laughing, reckless, and alive in the warmth of my friends' company. I hadn't felt that way since I first ran away, since the war began, or since I became a mother. For a few hours, the weight slipped off my shoulders, and I remembered what it was like just to be me.

Before the night ended, Lilly pulled me aside, her eyes shining but heavy. She told me her husband had orders, and she'd be leaving soon. My heart sank. *No, not her.* I had just started to find a home again in my friends, in people who felt like family, perfect strangers who cared about me without judgment. And now she was leaving. She wasn't just my friend; she had become my best friend, something I never had before.

By the time I got home, no one even noticed I'd been gone. To my surprise, he was asleep on the floor, using a rolled-up blanket as a pillow. I slipped into bed quietly, holding onto the feeling from earlier, not wanting to let it go.

In the weeks that followed, I spent as much time with Lilly as I could, helping her pack her things, stalling the goodbye. I didn't realize until then just how much I leaned on her. On the nights he frightened me, I slept on her couch with my son curled beside me. When he took my keys, she handed me hers. When I needed someone, she was there.

That's what a real friend is: someone who shows up without keeping score, who makes space for you when the rest of the world feels too small.

She kept insisting we'd keep in touch. *We have phones. We have the internet. Everything will be fine.* But she was still young, still unscarred by the weight of goodbyes. I knew better.

She came by one last time. The baby was asleep, so she stepped outside for our goodbye. She bent down, hugged my son, and whispered for him to be good. Then she turned to me and just stared like she was trying to memorize my face. I fought with everything in me not to pout.

Finally, she pulled me into the kind of hug that feels like a plea. Her whole body shook as she cried into my shoulder. *"I'm going to miss you,"* she sobbed. I held her as tightly as I could, as if maybe I could keep her there. Time stretched. And then, too soon, she let go.

She climbed into the car, shutting the door with a sound that felt final. I couldn't bring myself to say anything else. I hadn't realized goodbyes would still hurt this much; that the older I got, the sharper they cut, because I understood them more.

She turned to check the baby in the back seat, then looked up at me and waved softly. I waved back, all the while trying to remain steady in front of my son. But she turned her face forward, answered the call of an Army wife, and drove away. My son and I stood there holding hands, watching her for as long as we could until her car disappeared from view.

"Where's she goin'? he asked. "Far away".

Our time as friends had been completed.

Starting Over

I wandered through the vast building, its endless hallways and countless doors unfolding like a maze. Outside, the landscape was so grand it felt like the grounds of a king's palace in Versailles.
Inside, people of every age and race moved with purpose, gathering at scattered tables in the open lobby, their eyes fixed on books and notes as if filling their minds with treasure.
What is this place? I wondered.

It was college.

No one had ever talked to me about college before. Shamefully, I didn't even know what people did there. I thought it was only for those training to become doctors or lawyers, people who were nothing like me. I never imagined it could be within my reach.

A therapist I was seeing encouraged me to get my GED. I didn't understand why it mattered at the time, but I did it anyway. I finished night school. So many setbacks, and so many "life happens" moments, and now there I was. Starting a new beginning.
I realized I didn't have to live just to survive. I didn't have to keep running. I could choose something else.

When I finally walked into my first college classroom, I had no plan, no certainty, and no guarantee I would succeed. I didn't have the strong high school foundation that so many others relied on. I started at the very bottom, swimming upstream with everything I had.

At the same time, I was raising two children. I was broke, exhausted, and carrying the weight of work, school, and motherhood all at once. I worked part-time at a coffee shop and a library, spending much of my earnings to pay family members to watch my kids. I didn't have a village. I just had myself.

The three of us shared a single small room in a mobile home that sat in a dusty trailer park, with a cat. Every morning, we'd take the long way to school so we could talk and play. In the afternoons, we'd walk home down the street with the Thundercloud trees, stopping to pick summer plums from trees that blossomed like pink clouds. On those paths, we felt like royalty.

But the back-and-forth with their dad weighed heavily on me. I hated the instability. I hated knowing it hurt them. It made me feel inadequate—a constant reminder of a chapter I wished I could rewrite. To this day, I still cry about it.

And yet, I kept going. It wasn't easy. It took some time. But I finished college. I kept my promise.

Today, I help people heal—emotionally and physically. And in a way, I learned to heal myself.

I became a nurse.

It's a Short Walk to the Moon

At night, walking the path led to the end of a trailer park where there were no trees standing, and you could see the moon as vibrant as ever, gleaming down on just me.

I hadn't dated again. Not yet. I never knew what was capable, now that I was alone with two kids in tow. I never had that kind of companion. I didn't know how it worked. I wasn't running away, so…what *did* normal couples do?

I learned the hard way. And some lessons are only learned that way. There are boys and there are men. And some are just the devil in disguise.

I looked up at that moon, the same moon that looked down at my big shining eyes as a child, the same moon that witnessed so much pain, the same moon that lit my room when we had no lights on.

I took a walk to clear my head. I was naïve and hopeful. I didn't know who I was anymore or what my place was. I didn't know how to be an adult. All I knew was that nearly every adult had hurt me in some way, and I was afraid to socialize since.

I met a boy or two. They wouldn't last. They would cause more pain and chaos.

I was oblivious at times. But the walk to the moon was great, and it was hard to let that go. I believed in something. I wanted to.

And getting broken doesn't get easier. But some people are there just to hitch a ride. And what I left wasn't just sorrow and brokenness. It was a lesson in patience and trust. And how to guard my heart.

And that heathen on that road didn't stay long, and I appreciate that the most. No ties. No intertwined relations. Just the brevity of lessons learned from wolves in sheep's clothing.

It was a short walk to that moon.

When You Know, You Know

For a long time, I carried the quiet truth that I had never truly been in love. There had been fleeting sparks, dates that ended in disappointment, heartbreaks that left me hollow, lessons carved deep by people who came and went. I knew the ache of love gone wrong, but not the steady warmth of love being right.

In poems and paintings, in theater and film, love always seemed like an enchantment, with two souls caught in a shared spell, moving through the world as if lit from within. I had seen so many versions of it in art. But in life, I only knew what love was *not*.

It was not one-sided.
It was not begging to be chosen.
It was not the kind of hurt that repeats itself, followed by endless apologies that never change a thing.

What I didn't know yet was what love *is*.

Before I could find it, I had to find myself. I had to strip away the layers of pain and the distorted image I saw in the mirror. I had to believe I was worthy of something real—something safe—before I could ever let it in. If I didn't, I would keep settling for scraps, believing that's all I deserved.

I grew up in a world where love was often laced with cruelty. My parents fought in ways that bruised more than just walls. My father's voice spoke bitterly about my mother; my mother's words painted my father as villainous. I was the quiet witness, caught in the crossfire.

Beyond my parents' door, it was no different. I saw my aunts endure hurt from men who claimed to love them. I saw my cousins flinch under the weight of their parents' anger. Weddings were something I had only seen in movies. I didn't know a single couple who was married.

When I grew up, I told myself I didn't want a boyfriend. I didn't want the drama, the chaos, the slow erosion of tenderness I had watched my whole life.

And yet… deep in some fragile, hidden part of me, I still wanted more. I wanted a place like a pillow to rest my head forever. A heart I could trust to hold mine gently.

Then I met him.

And I knew.

Without question, without doubt, without even understanding why—I felt safe. Truly safe, in a way I never had before. And in that moment, I understood: For me, safety was love.
And love meant always feeling safe.

Run With Me

Over the years, I've walked away from situations unsure of what tomorrow would look like, afraid of the future, afraid of the present, afraid of the unknown, but I still walked away. And I kept going. Even when it hurt.

Leaving was something I learned early on. It became my comfort zone. My way of staying steady in the only kind of life I'd ever known. It was the only remedy I learned to patch up a broken world.

But I have him now.

And suddenly, every heartbreak, every mistake, every goodbye makes sense. He is my calm in the storm, the boy's jacket I slip under when it rains, the one I share my hot dog with at the game, my forever stolen hoodie, always warm, always mine.

We have each other. Wherever, whenever, we go together. Almost like God knew I would need someone willing to escape reality sometimes, without question. He knew me.

I am a soldier's wife. Our lives are all about leaving. When before, I would leave out of loss or failure, I don't anymore.

I leave with my head held high, with little to nothing but the clothes on my back…and his hand in my hand.

I Love You Too

The pain, the laughs, the silly little things I remembered enough to share, they weren't always easy to talk about. I went through a season of forgiving myself and throwing out the trash. Nothing dramatic, nothing anyone else would find remarkable. Just… healing. Quietly.

Some stories I love to tell. Others are too painful to remember, let alone relive. Then, there are the stories I'll never tell. There are things I wish I could erase, things I wish had never happened. There are some people not worthy to be written about.

Sometimes I wish I could hug my old self—the one in that picture, perched on a pony, no older than a toddler. My face is full of awe, eyes wide with wonder at the world, completely oblivious of the difficult road ahead. My dad kneels just behind the horse, hidden from view, ready to catch me if I fall. And even now, I can't help but wonder why he stopped.

I want to wrap my arms around her and whisper: "You are a beautiful person. When you feel hungry, God will find a way to feed you."
"When you are cold and afraid, and your mama isn't there, look up and know that He is."

But I'm not a preacher.

So, I'd just hug me tight and say, I love you.

I love you, too.

Man in The Moon

I followed you at night from the backseat of the car,

I saw you looking at me, just wondering how far.

The night was at its peak when I saw you look out,

Gazing at my shadows, I might have seen you pout.

You woke up in the twilight once and didn't know what you wanted.

You said you couldn't sleep because your dreams made you feel haunted.

I looked down at your face one night, and a diamond seemed to fall.

I watched you talk up to the stars, who, with me, watched it all.

You couldn't see me on this occasion, but know that I was there.
When you gave your heart to someone, and the whole world seemed so fair.

And when you let him hold you tight, you peeked at me over his shoulder,

And did this many other nights as I watched you grow older.

And when you held your infant close, to see his first night sky,

You wished to me that time could stop, then sang a lullaby.

The world was not so fair, after all, and I watched you sing alone.

Undeserving of the cruelty that the people you loved had shown.

The air was crisp and cool one fall, and I rose to my best light,

The same colors blanketed your world on your harvest moon birth night.

And I watched you gain and lose control, and grow up way too soon.

I wane or wax, I love you so, for I am the man in the moon.

I am the man in the moon.